Einar Thomassen
The Coherence of "Gnosticism"

Hans-Lietzmann-Vorlesungen

―

Edited on behalf of the Berlin-Brandenburg Academy
of Sciences and Humanities
by Katharina Bracht and Christoph Markschies

Volume 18

Einar Thomassen

The Coherence of "Gnosticism"

DE GRUYTER

Akademieunternehmen „Die alexandrinische und antiochenische Bibelexegese in der Spätantike – Griechische Christliche Schriftsteller" der Berlin-Brandenburgischen Akademie der Wissenschaften

ISBN 978-3-11-070571-3
e-ISBN (PDF) 978-3-11-070582-9
e-ISBN (EPUB) 978-3-11-070589-8
ISSN 1861-6011

Library of Congress Control Number: 2020947882

Bibliographic information published by the Deutsche Nationalbibliothek
The Deutsche Nationalbibliothek lists this publication in the Deutsche Nationalbibliografie; detailed bibliographic data are available on the Internet at http://dnb.dnb.de.

© 2021 Walter de Gruyter GmbH, Berlin/Boston
Printing and binding: CPI books GmbH, Leck

www.degruyter.com

Preface

The twenty-fourth Hans Lietzmann Lecture was held in 2018 by the Norwegian historian of religion Einar Thomassen and it is my great pleasure to be able to present it here in print. With the Hans Lietzmann Lecture, the "Greek Christian Writers" project established by Adolf Harnack at the Berlin-Brandenburg, formerly Prussian Academy of Sciences, commemorates its second director, the historian of Christianity Hans Lietzmann, who worked in Jena and Berlin and died seventy-eight years ago after a serious illness shortly before he was to retire.[1] But the venerable Berlin-based project is just one of the organising parties, and, from a historical perspective, one of the latter ones to join those ranks: Friedrich Schiller University in Jena, Humboldt University in Berlin and the Berlin-Brandenburg Academy of Sciences and Humanities, where Lietzmann was professor and head of the Commission for the History of Late-Antiquity Religion, also take part in honouring Lietzmann through the lecture. These institutions do not so much honour a person, however, who in some ways naturally appears quite foreign to us today, but rather his academic work on the history of religion of the Roman imperial period and late antiquity, which was both methodologically broad, drawing on texts as well as archaeological artefacts, and comprehensive with respect to the philological and cultural-historical

---

[1] Heinrich Bornkamm, "Hans Lietzmann zum Gedächtnis." *Die Antike* 19 (1943), 81–85; Johannes Stroux, "Gedächtnisrede auf Hans Lietzmann." In Deutsche Akademie der Wissenschaften (eds.), *Jahrbuch der Deutschen Akademie der Wissenschaften zu Berlin 1946–1949* (Berlin: Akademie-Verlag 1950), 183–191; Kurt Aland, *Glanz und Niedergang der deutschen Universität: 50 Jahre deutsche Wissenschaftsgeschichte in Briefen an und von Hans Lietzmann (1892–1942)* (Berlin/New York: De Gruyter 1979), 1–155 and 1194–1222; Wolfram Kinzig, "Evangelische Patristiker und Christliche Archäologen im 'Dritten Reich'. Drei Fallstudien: Hans Lietzmann, Hans von Soden, Hermann Wolfgang Beyer." In Beat Näf (ed.), *Antike und Altertumswissenschaft in der Zeit von Faschismus und Nationalsozialismus* (Texts and Studies in the History of Humanities 1; Mandelbachtal/Cambridge: edition Cicero 2001), 535–629 and ibid., "Hans Lietzmann (1875–1942)." In Reinhard Schmidt-Rost, Stephan Bitter, Martin Dutzmann (eds.), *Theologie als Vermittlung. Bonner evangelische Theologen des 19. Jahrhunderts im Porträt* (Arbeiten zur Theologiegeschichte 6; Rheinbach: cmz 2003), 220–231. – In print: Christoph Markschies, *Kirchenhistoriker als Herausgeber der "Theologischen Literaturzeitung". Erwägungen zu Geschichte, Gegenwart und Zukunft einer Rezensionszeitschrift* (Theologische Literaturzeitung. Forum; Leipzig: Evangelische Verlagsanstalt 2020) with extensive commentaries on Lietzmann as the chairman of the advisory council and editor of the *Theologische Literaturzeitung*.

contexts. It is as relevant today as it was decades ago when Lietzmann developed it as a student of Hermann Usener in Bonn and later brought it to completion in Jena and Berlin.²

Although only seventeen booklets of this lecture series have been published to date – as latest publications Jörg Rüpke on "Religiöse Transformationen im römischen Reich" [Religious Transformations in the Roman Empire] and Wolfram Kinzig on "Das Apostolische Glaubensbekenntnis" [The Apostolic Creed], i.e. the lectures from 2015 and 2017, respectively, as always by the publisher to which Hans Lietzmann was also particularly close, the Berlin publisher De Gruyter –, a total of twenty-three lectures had already been held by the time Thomassen gave his address.³ The anniversary event marking the twenty-fifth lecture was accordingly held in 2019. Over the first ten years of this lecture series, the foreword to the published lectures invariably made reference to an anonymous text on the theological principles of arithmetic, the *Theologumena arithmeticae*,⁴ as a means of establishing links between the number of the lecture, the topic and the lecturer. Soon this was no longer possible, as the work ends with the decade, the number ten. With respect to Einar Thomassen, an internationally leading scholar on the history of religion in antiquity, it would have been delightful if the unknown author of late antiquity had taken the count somewhat further and gone beyond the number 10.⁵ After all, the Neopythagorean number theory and speculation are by no means unfamiliar to the Norwegian religious scholar; quite the contrary. Neopythagoreanism and Middle Platonism are absolutely central to a certain subset of his works: With his reference to the Neopythagorean Moderatus of Gades (in today's Jordan: ὁ ἐκ

---

2 This contemporary aspect is also documented by the various issues of this lecture series, each of which refers to Lietzmann's program and his accomplishments in a different manner.

3 A useful compilation of the topics and the published issues can be found on the homepage of the chair of Professor Katharina Bracht in Jena: https://www.theologie.uni-jena.de/Lietzmann_Vorlesung_Jena.html or on the homepage of Christoph Markschies: https://www.antikes-christentum.de/de/profil/hans-lietzmann-vorlesungen/ (last retrieved on July 31, 2020).

4 [Iamblichi], *Theologumena Arithmeticae*, ed. Victorius de Falco (BiTeu; Leipzig: Teubner 1922); *The Theology of Arithmetic*, translated by Robin Waterfield with a Foreword by Keith Critchlow (Grand Rapids, MI: Phanes Press 1988).

5 For these purposes, one would have to directly apply the Neopythagorean and Neoplatonic mathematical and number theory, as found for example in Theon of Smyrna in his *Expositio rerum mathematicarum* and also look at Nicomachus of Gerasa via Iamblichus. For the number 24 see: *Theon Smyrnaei Philosophi Platonici Expositio Rerum Mathematicarum ad Legendum Platonem Vtilivm*, recensuit Eduardus Hiller (BiTeu; Stuttgart/Leipzig: Teubner 1995 = 1878), p. 28,2.

Γαδείρων⁶), which was recently edited and translated once again by Marie-Luise Lakmann, Einar Thomassen was the first to consult a philosopher concerning the explanation of the Valentinian Gnosis who was not only interested in number theory like (Pseudo-)Iamblichus, but who, with his specific theory of principles, displayed astonishing parallels to the "Valentinian" form of the gnostic theory of principles and cosmology examined in such detail by Thomassen.[7] So although it would be very nice to be able to establish a link between the ordinal number of this lecture and the Neopythagorean tradition once again, unfortunately that will not be possible. Alas, the number twenty-four does not play an independent role either in Neopythagoreanism or the Valentinian Gnosis – eight, ten, twelve and thirty are the critical numbers for the "eternities", the aeons.

As this introduction has already established, Einar Thomassen, born in Bergen in 1951 and raised in the Laksevåg district of the old Norwegian Hanseatic city, possesses a formidable philological education and is conversant with non-Christian antiquity, the Coptic-Gnostic texts as well as early, medieval and modern Islam. At the Bergen Cathedral School he received instruction not only in Latin and Greek, but was also introduced to the Coptic language. His scientific career would also take him away from Bergen quite early on: he studied both in his home country (where he obtained a master's degree) and in Sweden, France and Scotland, where he received his Ph.D. at St Andrews in 1982 with a dissertation on a text from the Nag Hammadi site. After a stint as a research assistant in Bergen (1982-1986), Thomassen first taught as a lecturer in Uppsala (1986-1990) and then as an associate professor in Oslo (1990-1992). From 1993 he has been Professor Professor for Religious Studies at the university in Bergen, his hometown, and in 2004 he was admitted to the Norwegian Academy of

---

[6] Franco Ferrari, "§ 66. Moderatus von Gades." In Christoph Riedweg, Christoph Horn, and Dietmar Wyrwa (eds.), *Philosophie der Kaiserzeit und der Spätantike* (Grundriss der Geschichte der Philosophie. Die Philosophie der Antike. Vol. 5/1; Basel: Schwabe 2018), 639–641.

[7] Einar Thomassen, *The Spiritual Seed. The Church of the "Valentinians"* (NHMS 60; Leiden/Boston: Brill 2006), 271–275; the famous lecture about the principle teachings and the genesis of material can also be found with a commentary in Heinrich Dörrie/Matthias Baltes, *Die philosophische Lehre des Platonismus. Einige grundlegende Axione / Platonische Physik (im antiken Verständnis) I. Bausteine 101–124: Text, Übersetzung und Kommentar* (Der Platonismus in der Antike. Grundlagen – System – Entwicklung, Vol. 4; Stuttgart-Bad Cannstatt: Frommann-Holzboog 1996), p. 176–179 (Baustein 122.1). 473–477 (= Simpl., In Arist. Phys. p. 230,34–231,24 Diels) and now Marie-Luise Lakmann, *Platonici Minores: 1. Jh. v. Chr. – 2. Jh. n. Chr. Prosopographie. Fragmente und Testimonien mit deutscher Übersetzung* (Philosophia Antiqua 145; Leiden/Boston: Brill, 2016), 183–190. 618–629 as well as Christian Tornau, "Die Prinzipienlehre des Moderatos von Gades." *Rheinisches Museum für Philologie* 143 (2000) 197–220.

Sciences. Many colleagues remember him fondly as the Vice President and President of the European Association for the Study of Religion (2010-2013 and 2014-2019, respectively). He has also worked tirelessly to bring the work of Norwegian religious studies to other academic contexts (and vice versa, to make the results of research in his home country more widely known).[8]

The research and teaching of Einar Thomassen are characterised by the fact that he represents the field of general religious studies and the history of religion with exceptional breadth – beyond his historical works, which span a lengthy period from antiquity to the early Middle Ages and include Islamic forms[9] of religion in addition to pagan and Christian forms, he has also published work on methodology and the profile of the field.[10] He is also interested in comparative questions, in conjunction with insights from the fields of cognitive psychology and evolution theory. What makes Thomassen particularly interesting for a Hans Lietzmann Lecture is naturally not only his publications on the religious history of antiquity, the pre-Islamic Middle East and the methodology of religious studies, but above all his works on Gnosis and Gnosticism. Thomassen has published commanding contributions to this particular area of the history of the religion of antiquity; particularly noteworthy in this regard are his works on the Valentinian Gnosis[11] and the library find of Nag Hammadi. Editions

---

8 See, for example, Mircea Eliade, *Det hellige og det profane og andre skrifter*. Oversatt av Trond Berg Eriksen, Øyunn Hestetun og Einar Thomassen, innledende essay av Einar Thomassen (Bokklubbens kulturbibliotek; Oslo: De norske bokklubbene 2003).

9 *The letters of Aḥmad Ibn Idrīs*. Ed., transl. and annot. by Albrecht Hofheinz, General editor Einar Thomassen (Series in Islam and Society in Africa; Evanston, Ill.: Northwestern Univ. Press 1993); Einar Thomassen, "Review: The Qur'an: A New Annotated Translation by Arthur J. Droge, Bristol 2013." *Marburg Journal of Religion* 20 (2018), https://doi.org/10.17192/ mjr.2018.20.7943 (last retrieved on July 31, 2020).

10 For chapters on methodology, see for example: Einar Thomassen, "Is Magic a Subclass of Ritual?" In David R. Jordan (ed.), *The World of Ancient Magic* (Papers from the Norwegian Institute at Athens 4; Athens: Det Norske Institutt i Athen for Klassiske Studier, Arkeologi og Kulturhistorie 1999), 55–66; ibid. "What is a 'God' Actually?" In Peter Antes, Armin W. Geertz, Mikael Rothstein (eds.), *Contemporary Views on Comparative Religion in Celebration of Tim Jensen's 65th Birthday* (Sheffield: Equinox 2016), 365–374; ibid., "Review Symposium: Are Gods really Moral Monitors? Some Comments on Ara Norenzayan's Big Gods by a Historian of Religions." *Religion* (2014) 1–7 and Einar Thomassen (ed.), *Canon and Canonicity: The Formation and Use of Scripture* (Copenhagen: Museum Tusculanum Press 2010).

11 In excerpt: Thomassen, *The Spiritual Seed. The Church of the "Valentinians"*; ibid., "Valentinian Ideas about Salvation as Transformation." In Turid Karlsen Seim and Jorunn Økland (eds.), *Metamorphoses. Resurrection, Body and Transformative Practices in Early Christianity* (Ekstasis: Religious Experience from Antiquity to the Middle Ages 1; Berlin/New York: De Gruyter 2009), 169–186; ibid., "Heracleon." In Tuomas Rasimus (ed.), *The Legacy of John.*

of texts from this library find amply demonstrate his coptological expertise.[12] His latest, comprehensive work on the subject, was recently published: the respective section in the new "Ueberweg", the trilogy on the Roman imperial period and late antiquity with regard to the foundations of the history of philosophy.[13] A commemorative publication acknowledges his importance as a scholar in the field of the Gnosis of antiquity;[14] it is noteworthy in this regard that the honouree is at home and well respected in both the Francophone and Anglophone communities of Nag Hammadi research.

As a student of the classic philologist and scholar of religious studies Hermann Usener, Hans Lietzmann almost certainly had a strong interest in matters of religious history while, as a Protestant theologian, the theory of secular religious studies hardly interested him at all. He had already examined publications about Gnosticism early on in critiques,[15] but the thus designated movements definitely were not the main focus of his research work. Before the First World War, he worked a great deal with considerably later texts like the catenae

---

Second-century Reception of the Fourth Gospel (NT.S 132; Leiden/Boston 2010), 173–210; ibid., "Baptism among the Valentinians." In David Hellholm, Tor Vegge, Oyvind Norderval, Christer Hellholm (eds.), *Ablution, Initiation, and Baptism: Late Antiquity, Early Judaism and Early Christianity*. Vol. 2 (BZNW 176/2; Berlin/New York: De Gruyter 2011), 895–916; ibid., "The Eucharist in Valentinianism." In David Hellholm, Dieter Sänger (eds.), *The Eucharist – Its Origins and Contexts. Sacred Meal, Communal Meal, Table Fellowship in Late Antiquity, Early Judaism, and Early Christianity*. Vol. 2 (WUNT 376; Tübingen: Mohr Siebeck 2017), 1833–1849; however, see also Christoph Markschies and Einar Thomassen (eds.), *Valentinianism: New Studies* (NHMS 96; Leiden/Boston: Brill 2019 and especially the Introduction by the editors: pp. 1–14.

12 Einar Thomassen, *The Tripartite Tractate from Nag Hammadi. A New Translation with Introduction and Commentary*. 2 Vols. (PhD St Andrews, 1980/1982); *Le traité tripartite (NH I,5)*. Texte établi, introd. et commenté par Einar Thomassen (BCNH. Section Textes 19; Québec: Les Presses de l'Université Laval 1989); *L'interprétation de la Gnose (NH XI,1)*. Texte établi, introd. et commenté par Wolf-Peter Funk, Louis Painchaud et Einar Thomassen (BCNH. Section Textes 34; Québec: Les Presses de l'Université Laval 2010).

13 Einar Thomassen, "III. Gnostizismus und Verwandtes." In Christoph Riedweg, Christoph Horn, and Dietmar Wyrwa (eds.), *Philosophie der Kaiserzeit und der Spätantike* (Grundriss der Geschichte der Philosophie. Die Philosophie der Antike. Bd 5/2; Basel: Schwabe 2018), 855–882.

14 Christian H. Bull, Liv Ingeborg Lied and John D. Turner (eds.), *Mystery and Secrecy in the Nag Hammadi Collection and Other Ancient Literature: Ideas and Practices. Studies for Einar Thomassen at Sixty* (NHMS 76; Leiden/Boston: Brill 2012).

15 Firstly: Hans Lietzmann, "Review Erwin Preuschen, Die Apokryphen gnostischen Adamschriften aus dem Armenischen übersetzt und untersucht, Gießen 1900." *Deutsche Literaturzeitung* 12 (1901) 2054–2056. A short piece deals with: "Gnosis und Magie." *Forschungen und Fortschritte* 9 (1933) 154f. = ibid., *Kleine Schriften I: Studien zur spätantiken Religionsgeschichte* (Texte und Untersuchungen 67; Berlin: Akademie 1958), 84–86.

and Byzantine vitae of the saints, and then increasingly also on liturgical questions. After the war, these areas of study were increasingly added to by archaeological questions and New Testament textual criticism.[16] Lietzmann seldom expressed himself generally about religion or even about religious studies;[17] he was obviously less interested in theoretical and methodological matters. More significant was the work he did on the question of the religious classification of the Mandaeans; his famous and many times reprinted *Beitrag zur Mandäerfrage* dismantled one of the fundamental key assumptions by the school of religious studies concerning the relationship between the canonical New Testament and Gnosticism. The view he elaborated in the book, that there were no Mandaeans in East Jordan at the time of Jesus and the early congregations, and that they are therefore not relevant to the emergence of the canonical gospels and any explanation of them, has prevailed.[18] It was, however, of great importance for the field of Gnostic research that Lietzmann – as Chairman of the Commission for Late Antique Religious History (or "for the study of church and religious history in the Roman imperial period") at the Prussian Academy of the Sciences (a position he took over from Harnack) – promoted the publication of the Berlin sections of the Coptic Manichaica with a great deal of energy.[19]

The most extensive comments by Lietzmann on the subject can be found in the first volume of his *Geschichte der Alten Kirche* (History of the Early Church)

---

16 In this context: Hans Lietzmann, "Ein Gnostiker in der Novatianuskatakombe." *Rivista di archeologia cristiana* 11 (1934) 359–362 = ibid., *Kleine Schriften I: Studien zur spätantiken Religionsgeschichte* (Texte und Untersuchungen 67; Berlin: Akademie 1958), 475–478.
17 Hans Lietzmann, "Religion." In Eduard Norden (ed.), *Vom Altertum zur Gegenwart. Die Kulturzusammenhänge in den Hauptepochen und auf den Hauptgebieten* (Berlin/Leipzig: Teubner 1919), 193–200. The piece appeared in a second, extended publication in Auflage 1921 (p. 258–267). See also ibid., "Religionswissenschaft und Religionsunterricht." In *Wirtschaft und Idealismus. Alfred Giesecke, dem Mitinhaber der Verlagsbuchhandlung B. G. Teubner zum 60. Geburtstag gewidmet* (Leipzig: Teubner 1928), 57–67. From 1933 onwards, Lietzmann also co-edited the "Archiv für Religionswissenschaft".
18 Hans Lietzmann, "Ein Beitrag zur Mandäerfrage." In *Sitzungsberichte der Preußischen Akademie der Wissenschaften* Nr. 27 (1930) (Berlin: De Gruyter 1930) = ibid., *Kleine Schriften I: Studien zur spätantiken Religionsgeschichte* (Texte und Untersuchungen 67; Berlin: Akademie 1958), 124–140.
19 James M. Robinson, *The Manichaean Codices of Medinet Madi* (Eugene, OR: Cascade 2013), passim; Alexander Böhlig, "Neue Initiativen zur Erschließung der koptisch-manichäischen Bibliothek von Medinet Madi." ZNW 80 (1989) 240–262; Siegfried G. Richter, "The Coptic Manichaean Library from Madinat Madi in the Fayoum." In Gawdat Gabra (ed.), *Christianity and Monasticism in the Fayoum Oasis. Essays from the 2004 International Symposium of the Saint Mark Foundation and the Saint Shenouda the Archimandrite Coptic Society in Honor of Martin Krause* (Cairo/New York: The American University in Cairo Press 2005), 71–78.

from the year 1932.[20] The chapter at the end of this volume was, for example, sharply criticized in a commentary by Rudolf Bultmann – but questions concerning a Gnostic understanding of being as posed by Bultmann and his master student Hans Jonas were of course completely alien to Lietzmann.[21] Lietzmann understood Gnosticism as a pagan movement, "which, emerging around the beginning of the Roman imperial era, increasingly dominated the first three centuries of our calendar. In the 2nd century, it joined forces with Christianity and created the great systems of Basilides and Valentinus which had a very strong influence on the Church through opposition and parallel development."[22] As such, his picture was not particularly original, but one can at least say that it was arrived at independently, to the extent that he always saw a link between archaeological artefacts and the so-called magical gems, as well as a connection between the so-called magical papyri and further magical texts with their originally pagan and syncretistic Gnosis. Lietzmann hoped to clarify precisely how the gems, the magical papyri and the Gnostic cosmogenies (or groups) were connected by carrying out further research and, for this purpose, he made efforts to bring together as extensive as possible a collection of plaster casts in the highly traditional Christian archaeological collection of the theological faculty in Berlin.[23] Unfortunately this part of the collection, like so many other pieces, became lost during the war (and presumably during relocation), meaning that we cannot give any reliable information anymore about the size and quality of this collection.[24] Lietzmann's early death prevented further work from being carried out in this field.

Our picture has, of course, completely changed, at the latest after the discovery of the Nag Hammadi texts – and we are very grateful to Einar Thomassen for his extensive work on these. The contemporary picture we have of "Valentinianism" also has little to do with the entertaining retelling of a Valentinian mythology in Lietzmann's *A History of the Early Church*.[25] The Berlin church historian overlooked the references to Platonic teaching, recognizing only the

---

20 Hans Lietzmann, *Geschichte der Alten Kirche*. Vol. I Die Anfänge (Berlin: De Gruyter 1932 = ebd. 1999, with a preface by Christoph Markschies), 282–317.
21 Rudolf Bultmann, "Review Hans Lietzmann." *Zeitschrift für Kirchengeschichte* 53 (1934), 624 – 630, here 629 = ibid., Theologie als Kritik. Ausgewählte Rezensionen und Forschungsberichte (Tübingen: Mohr Siebeck 2002), 293–299, here 298.
22 Lietzmann, "Gnosis und Magie." 154 = 84.
23 Lietzmann, "Gnosis und Magie." 155 = 86.
24 References and literature on: https://www.sammlungen.hu-berlin.de/sammlungen/christlich-archaeologische-sammlung/ (last retrieved on July 31, 2020).
25 Lietzmann, *Geschichte der Alten Kirche*. Vol. I Die Anfänge, 309–314.

allusions to biblical texts. Irrespective of how one reconstructs the history of what is known as Valentinian Gnosticism, and no matter how one feels about the masterly reconstruction of "Valentinianism" by Einar Thomassen – it certainly remains important, particularly in view of the research consensus today, not to overlook the elements of magical piety and pagan religiosity in the description of Gnosticism in religious studies. As such, Lietzmann's to a great extent outdated picture of Gnosticism still retains a certain importance.

Einar Thomassen presented a remarkable composition of his various works and expanded on them again for publication. That is something we must thank him for, but also for the fact that he accepted an invitation to a city in which an occupation of Norway by German troops was planned, the bitter consequences of which also affected his family. The international exchange within the scientific community on the one hand, and the critical remembrance of the past on the other can help to prevent repetitions of such terrible periods in European and German history. These are also reasons why Lietzmann is remembered in Jena and Berlin. Once again, our thanks go to the De Gruyter publishing house for their great cooperation and publication, and for sponsoring the event; the coordination with my colleague and co-editor Katharina Bracht was also excellent. My assistant Philipp Pilhofer was kind enough to proof the manuscript for errors during a very special period, which I cordially thank him for.

Berlin, July 2020   Christoph Markschies

Table of Contents

Preface —— V

1   **Is it still possible to speak about "Gnosticism"?** —— 1

2   **Reconstructing coherence** —— 5

3   **Valentinus and "the Gnostic sect"** —— 6

4   **Irenaeus, *Haer*. 1.29 and the *Apocryphon of John*** —— 10

5   **The mythological system of Irenaeus, *Haer*. 1.29** —— 13

6   **The protologies of *Haer*. 1.29 and 1.30 compared** —— 18

7   **The Valentinian reception of Gnostic protology** —— 21
          Ennoia – the Thought —— 21
          The Primordial Anthropos —— 23
          Sophia and Christos —— 25

8   **The underlying logic of Gnostic protology** —— 26

9   **Conclusion** —— 34

Bibliography —— 37

1 Is it still possible to speak about "Gnosticism"?

The assumption that there existed in Antiquity a religious movement called "Gnosticism" was long taken for granted. Although the name "Gnosticism" is itself a relatively modern invention,[1] generations of scholars, from the 18th century onwards, were rarely in doubt that it referred to a genuine and distinct historical phenomenon. It was also taken for granted that that phenomenon essentially corresponded to what Irenaeus of Lyons in his *Adversus haereses*, the earliest preserved account of Christian heresies, referred to as "the falsely called knowledge". Following the ancient heresiologists, scholars of the 18th and 19th centuries usually treated Gnosticism as a chapter in the history of the early Church, either as an aberrant interpretation of Christianity against which "the Church" had to defend itself in order to be faithful to the authentic message of the Gospel; or, more sympathetically, as the earliest attempt to give Christianity a philosophical or a mystical interpretation. At the same time, ambiguity prevailed as to whether the Gnostic phenomenon had originated within Christianity itself or had crept into the early Church from the outside. The latter assumption gave rise to a number of theories that sought to locate the origins of Gnosticism in a non-Christian environment, either in "Oriental" religions, in Greek philosophy or religion, or in some form of heterodox Judaism. Especially influential, for a while, was the so-called *Religionsgeschichtliche Schule* (Bousset, Reitzenstein, and others), which regarded Gnosticism as a pre-Christian religious movement whose origins lay in Mesopotamia and/or Iran. Notwithstanding the disagreements over the origins of the phenomenon, scholars generally shared the conviction that Gnosticism represented a distinctive religious attitude, a religion *sui generis*. It was common to speak about "the essence of Gnosticism".

This conviction was still prevalent at the historic conference on "The Origins of Gnosticism" held in Messina in April 1966,[2] although the leading scholars assembled there were unable in the end to produce a workable and universally accepted definition of "Gnosticism". In the following decades, research in this area was thoroughly transformed by the publication and intensive study of

---

[1] It is apparently first attested in 1664, in the works of the Cambridge Neoplatonist Henry More (*OED*). In French and German, the appellations *la gnose* and *die Gnosis* have been more commonly used than *gnosticisme* and *Gnostizismus*.
[2] Bianchi (ed.), *Le Origini dello gnosticismo*.

the some fifty new "Gnostic" texts discovered in the Nag Hammadi Library. The access to sources that were independent of the interpretive frames imposed by the heresiologists, and the growing appreciation of the diversity of the ideas found in them, led to a reconsideration of inherited categories. In addition, the general anti-essentialist turn in the epistemology of the humanities that emerged in that period had an impact on this field of study as well. As a result, the validity of the category of "Gnosticism" itself came to be questioned.

Many scholars are now of the opinion that the concept of "Gnosticism" should be abandoned altogether. They argue that the concept is unhelpful as a general category because the phenomena it is supposed to cover are too diverse to be brought under a common denominator. Thus, the concept lacks descriptive precision and has no explanatory power. Moreover, "Gnosticism" is a label that derives from the intolerant prejudice of the ancient heresiologists; it is therefore an ideologically loaded term that is unsuitable for proper historical analysis. A representative, some might say extreme, example of this current trend in scholarship is found in the "Report on Gnosticism" produced a few years ago by the Christianity Seminar of the Westar Institute – also home to the well-known Jesus Seminar.[3] With "at least twenty-five internationally known scholars in attendance", the final report concluded that, "[t]he category of gnosticism needs to be dismantled." This proposition was voted "Red" by the assembled scholars, a verdict which means that the seminar harboured no doubts about this matter. "[A]fter strong discussion of major papers", the report states, "the Seminar said clearly that most historians of the past 100+ years were wrong in thinking that such a phenomenon as 'Gnosticism' ever existed."

The chief argument for this claim is that the concept of Gnosticism is inextricably bound up with that of "heresy", which in turn presupposes the notion of "orthodoxy". It is inappropriate, however (the argument goes), to draw boundaries between orthodoxy and heresy in pre-Nicene Christianity. It is important not to confuse "the post-Constantinian project of creating a 'catholic' Church, characterized by uniform theologies, structures, and practices, with earlier Christian persons and groups". To avoid such anachronisms, one must also discard such expressions as "the Great Church," "(emerging) Catholicism", "mainstream Christianity", or "proto-orthodoxy". What we are left with, in the end, is simply a diversity of religious phenomena that in one way or another relate themselves to the figure of Jesus of Nazareth – "Jesus groups and Christ movements". Scholars should allow them all to be their authentic pre-Nicene

---

3 https://www.westarinstitute.org/projects/christianity-seminar/fall-2014-meeting-report/

selves, without having the labels of orthodox or heretical anachronistically forced upon them.

The current critique of "Gnosticism" as a category relies upon two books in particular that were published in the last couple of decades: Michael Williams's *Rethinking "Gnosticism"* (1996) and Karen King's *What is Gnosticism* (2003). Michael Williams' book was particularly critical of the stereotypical descriptions of the ancient Gnostics as deeply alienated souls who hated the world and their own bodies, who despised the creator of the cosmos who had imprisoned them in matter, and who, being convinced that they belonged to a spiritual race superior to other human beings, sought redemption either through extreme asceticism or transgressive libertinism. Williams argued that these stereotypes do not do justice to the diversity of ideas and attitudes that are attested in the original sources that are now available to us in the Nag Hammadi Library. Transgressive libertinism is not attested there at all, extreme asceticism is not typical, and attitudes to the cosmos and its creator vary considerably. Thus, what has conventionally been called "Gnosticism" was not a unitary phenomenon, and its manifold manifestations cannot be reduced to a common "essence". Karen King's book focused on how the blanket term "Gnosticism" has served as an instrument of exclusion, by defining groups and ideas as not Christian, heretical, and a "danger" that the early Church had to fight against in order to remain true to its authentic apostolic heritage.

The critique voiced by Williams and King has, without doubt, led to a higher level of reflection in this area of scholarship. We have become rather more conscious of the way in which the category "Gnosticism" has been pre-formed by ancient heresiology, and we no longer speak about "the essence of Gnosticism" as easily as scholars did a generation or two ago. This last point may be further illustrated by the following observations.

Attempts to define the "essence" of gnosis, or Gnosticism, regularly make use of a combination of criteria, which may be adequately summarised in four points:[4] (1) the idea that the material world, corporeal existence and the passions of the soul are evil and that liberation from these evils is the fundamental goal of salvation; (2) the distinction between a supreme deity and an inferior, more or less evil figure who is responsible for creating the cosmos and the human body and soul; (3) the idea that an inner, redeemable core in (some) humans is of the same substance as (is consubstantial with) the supreme divinity;

---

[4] A number of definitions and lists of criteria for "Gnosticism" and "Gnosis" have been proposed in earlier scholarship, many of them more detailed than the list offered here. For a general survey, see Lahe, *Gnosis und Judentum*, especially 11–53.

(4) the idea that redemption requires and is brought about by a certain type of knowledge, *gnosis*. The problem with this set of criteria is that each of the four themes can be found elsewhere, both in antiquity and in the history of religions at large. Thus, the "Gnostic" views of matter, the body, and the passions were widely shared by the ancient schools of philosophy. The same may be said about the idea of divine-human consubstantiality and that of the soteriological value of "knowledge". Theological dualism is found in Marcion in antiquity and among the medieval Cathars; neither of these, however, highlighted "knowledge" as the path to salvation.

Many more examples might be mentioned, but in view of the limitations of the present format, I shall move straight to the conclusion: the combination of these four themes within the compass of a single system of religious thought, such as can be found in the classic Gnostic systems reported by the church fathers, does not constitute a set of propositions that are inseparably connected by means of logically necessary mutual implications. Rather, their combination is a matter of historical contingency. In consequence, the themes do not add up to an "essence" whose instantiations may be recognised in different empirical contexts and which may thus serve as the basis for the definition of a general category. A further implication to be drawn from this observation is that we should refrain from referring to "Gnosticism" or "gnosis" whenever we encounter ideas about "knowledge" as a path to salvation, about the divine origins of the human soul or spirit, about a creator figure who is inferior to a supreme deity, or about the material world as evil. Too often, the presence of one of these ideas has been assumed to presuppose all the others, resulting in the indiscriminate use of the labels "gnosis" and "Gnostic" across cultures and historical periods, as well as in endless and futile debates as to whether a given document (e.g. the *Gospel of Thomas*), or a particular religious movement (e.g. Hermeticism), is to be regarded as "Gnostic" or not.

The current situation remains, however, rather paradoxical, in so far as the term continues to be used quite widely; a fresh example of this is Routledge's publication of *The Gnostic World*, which covers everything from gnosis in tribal cultures via ancient Gnosticism and Sufism, Shi'a Islam, Asian religions, Kabbalah, European esotericism, to Scientology and modern popular culture.[5] This highly generous understanding of "gnosis"[6] presents a striking contrast to the deconstructive scepticism expressed by those specialists who wish to abandon

---

[5] Trompf et al. (eds.), *The Gnostic World*.
[6] Other examples include Hanegraaff (ed.), *Dictionary of Gnosis & Western Esotericism*; DeConick, *The Gnostic New Age*.

the term altogether, or who accept its use only with reference to a very specific and apparently small group in antiquity that was referred to as "the *gnostikoi*", and possibly even adopted that name as their primary self-designation (a topic to which I shall return later).[7] To my mind, these wildly opposing ways of using the terms "gnosis" and "Gnosticism" are another indication that they have little or no informative value – they are terms that obscure and confuse our thinking more than they provide enlightenment.

2 Reconstructing coherence

If we must conclude that "gnosis" and "Gnosticism" are unhelpful as general categories because of their implicit essentialist and heresiological assumptions, we are faced with the challenge of finding other ways to discern coherence in the historical evidence preserved for us by the ancient heresiologists or rediscovered in such finds as the Nag Hammadi Library. It can hardly be satisfactory to regard the numerous theological ideas and positions attested in this material as simply individual varieties of early Christianity. We must certainly give up any ambition of characterising this material as a unit by means of essentialist formulas. But it is equally unhelpful to treat it merely as an arbitrary jumble of unconnected fragments. The deconstructive trend of the last couple of decades needs to be counterbalanced by new attempts at reconstructive historical synthesis that will detect coherence among a wider range of sources than current specialised scholarship is often disposed to acknowledge.

A project that aims to reconstruct a logic of historical development – an *Entwicklungslogik* – for certain clusters of ideas, even if restricted to parts of the evidence previously classified as "Gnostic", will first be confronted by the challenge of integrating the evidence of the patristic authors with that of the Nag Hammadi Codices. As is well known, a major difficulty posed by the texts from Nag Hammadi is the fact that these Coptic manuscripts, produced in the late fourth century, provide few indications as to when their original Greek versions may have been written. They do not supply the names of their human authors nor do they inform us about the milieus in which they originated. A further difficulty, to which we have now become increasingly sensitive, is the fact that this literature was typically fluid – texts were revised, improved upon, rewritten, and plagiarised in ways that can be reconstructed only to a very limited

---

7 E.g. Brakke, *The Gnostics*, following Layton, "Prolegomena".

extent by means of source critical ingenuity. For these reasons, only the writings of the church fathers, which can be dated with relative accuracy, will provide us with fixed points of reference. Any attempt to create chronological order and to trace historical developments must therefore take the patristic evidence as its point of departure.

3 Valentinus and "the Gnostic sect"

The most important piece of evidence of all in this regard is the work of Irenaeus of Lyons. Written in the 180s,[8] it is the earliest preserved account of ancient Christian "heresies". Irenaeus' treatise, whose precise title was *Exposure and refutation of the falsely called knowledge* (Ἔλεγχος καὶ ἀνατροπὴ τῆς ψευδωνύμου γνώσεως),[9] is also important because it, to a large extent, defined for posterity the category of "gnosis" and what it included. The main target of Irenaeus' attack on those who falsely claim "gnosis" was the followers of Valentinus. This he states explicitly in his preface to Book I, and the first two thirds of that book are devoted to an extensive report on the doctrines and the ritual practices of the Valentinians (*Haer.* 1.1–8; 1.11–21). A long-term effect of Irenaeus' perspective was that Valentinianism came to be perceived by scholars of the modern age as the prototypical example of "Gnosticism".

However, Irenaeus' notions about what constituted the Gnostic heresy are not unequivocal. On the one hand, he uses a wide concept of "gnosis" that includes much more than the Valentinians. In the final third of Book I he draws up a lineage of predecessors for the Valentinians, in which Simon Magus figures as the source and origin of all heresy (1.23–31). From this point of view, "the falsely called gnosis" of the Valentinians is just another manifestation of a larger heretical movement that began with the Samaritan heresiarch.[10] The idea of this heretical movement was constructed by Irenaeus on the basis of two authoritative apostolic texts in particular: the account of the confrontation be-

---

[8] The dating of Irenaeus' work was extensively studied by Harnack, *Geschichte der altchristlichen Litteratur*, I/1, 263–288. Harnack concluded that the work was written between 181 and 189. For further details, see Markschies, "Grande Notice", 38 n. 33.

[9] The title has been lost in the Latin manuscript transmission of Irenaeus' work (of the orginal Greek version only fragments are preserved, as quotations in other authors), but it is cited by Eusebius and several other ancient writers. See RD I/1, 31–35. In referring to this work I shall use the conventional abbreviation *Haer.*

[10] See in particular Brox, "Γνωστικοί", especially 108–11.

tween the apostles and Simon Magus in Acts 8, and the warning against "the falsely called gnosis" in 1 Tim 6:20. On the other hand, there also appears in Irenaeus a much narrower usage of the term "Gnostic", according to which "the Gnostics" is the name given to a specific group or movement within the greater mass of heretics.[11] The view that Irenaeus identifies a special group of *gnostikoi* in his work has become a common assumption in recent scholarship.[12] Furthermore, it is assumed that the doctrines of these "Gnostics" are to be found in the reports made by Irenaeus in the last chapters of Book I (chapters 29–31), and that Irenaeus regards them as the immediate predecessors of the Valentinians and the direct source of inspiration for Valentinus.

These assumptions are, in my opinion, well founded. A full discussion of the relevant evidence for them is beyond the scope of this lecture, but I shall discuss a couple of passages that are crucial for the argument that will be made later.

In one famous passage Irenaeus speaks about the source from which the school-founder Valentinus himself derived his teaching:

Ἴδωμεν νῦν καὶ τὴν τούτων ἄστατον γνώμην, δύο που καὶ τριῶν ὄντων πῶς περὶ τῶν αὐτῶν οὐ τὰ αὐτὰ λέγουσιν, ἀλλὰ τοῖς πράγμασι καὶ τοῖς ὀνόμασιν ἐναντία ἀποφαίνονται· Ὁ μὲν γὰρ πρῶτος, ἀπὸ τῆς λεγομένης γνωστικῆς αἱρέσεως τὰς ἀρχὰς εἰς ἴδιον χαρακτῆρα διδασκαλείου μεθαρμόσας Οὐαλεντῖνος, οὕτως ὡρίσατο·

Now let us also look at how unstable the doctrine of these people is, and how, as soon as there are two or three of them, they do not say the same things about the same subject, but contradict themselves in regard to things and names. Thus, the first of them, Valentinus, by adapting from the so-called Gnostic sect the principal ideas for his own distinctive school teaching, put forth the following: ... (1.11.1)

The passage is quoted here in full because the context for Irenaeus' statement is important: after having presented the intricate mythological system of the Valentinians in the first part of Book I, using as his main source a specific treatise he has been able to acquire (chapters 1–8), Irenaeus proceeds to describe the internal disagreements among the Valentinian teachers (chapters 11–12). He begins, naturally enough, with Valentinus himself, as the πρῶτος, "the first" (of

---

[11] RD II/1, 350–54 survey all the occurrences (around 15) of this usage in the five books of *Haer*.
[12] Cf. McGuire, "Valentinus"; Layton, "Prolegomena"; Edwards, "Gnostics and Valentinians", 26–30; Logan, *Gnostic Truth*, 1–10; Brakke, *Gnostics*, 31–35. This observation is not new; it was made already by Lipsius, *Quellen*, especially 219–21; cf. also Brox, "Γνωστικοί", 111–13. A recent dissenting view is represented by Schmid, *Christen und Sethianer*; "Valentinianer und 'Gnostiker'".

those Valentinian teachers)[13] and claims that Valentinus founded his school by taking over and adapting the prinicpal ideas of "the so-called Gnostic sect". This, Irenaeus implies, is how the Valentinian "school" began.

If Irenaeus is here using the expression "the so-called Gnostic sect", rather than "the Gnostics", which appears later in his work whenever he refers to this group, this is probably because he in this passage is mentioning the group for the first time. By saying "so-called" he is allowing for the possibility that the reader may not have heard of this group before.[14] The word *hairesis* is hardly to be understood as "sect" in the sense of a single community, since Irenaeus in chapters 29–31 speaks of several groups of *gnostikoi*.[15] *Hairesis* must therefore here be taken to mean a "school of thought", in the sense of a set of presuppositions shared by a certain number of people who from a sociological point of view exist as distinct groups.

---

13 Ὁ μὲν γὰρ πρῶτος must clearly be read in the context of τούτων in the previous sentence, which pronoun can only refer to the Valentinians, whose doctrines have been the subject matter of Irenaeus' entire exposition up to this point. No other heretical group has been mentioned so far. The immediately preceding text in 10.3 clearly alludes to the Valentinian doctrines reported in the previous chapters, and the expression οὗτοι οἱ ... διδάσκαλοι in that paragraph, the teachers who profess those doctrines, forms the specific reference for τούτων in 11.1. Moreover, ὁ μὲν γὰρ πρῶτος ... Οὐαλεντῖνος is followed by Σεκοῦνδος δὲ in 11.2 as the second Valentinian teacher whose doctrines Irenaeus is reporting. A different reading of the passage connects πρῶτος directly with ἀπὸ τῆς λεγομένης γνωστικῆς αἱρέσεως; thus Foerster in *Die Gnosis*, 1, 254: "Denn der erste von der sogenannten gnostischen Partei, der die Grundsätze zu einer eigenen Ausprägung der Lehre umwandelte, Valentinus ..."; cf. the English translation by David Hill in Foerster, *Gnosis, I*, 194: "Now the first of the so-called gnostic sect, the one who adopted the basic doctrines to his own individualistic brand of teaching, is Valentinus ...." Schmid, *Christen und Sethianer,* 221–22, and "Valentinianer und Gnostiker", defends this interpretation. It rests, however, on insufficient attention to the context of the passage. Moreover, it would not make much sense to present Valentinus as the first "Gnostic" to have developed his own doctrine when chapters 23–31 parade a series of predecessors of the Valentinians, each with their own distinctive teachings.
14 I tend to disagree with Brakke: "His [i.e. Irenaeus'] diction ... suggests that 'Gnostics' and 'Gnostic school of thought' functioned as proper names for the group" (*Gnostics*, 32; cf. also 46–49). Whereas being a "Gnostic" in the sense of "one who possesses knowledge" was undoubtedly an essential aspect of the self-understanding of the members of these groups, the use of this term as a name in referring to them is more likely to have been devised by outsiders. The implicit subject of λεγομένης is probably not the heretics themselves, but other Christians.
15 *Quidam enim eorum ... subiciunt* (1.29.1), *Alii autem rursus ... loquuntur* (1.30.1), *Alii autem rursus ... dicunt* (1.31.1).

Irenaeus then goes on to report the doctrine of "Valentinus".[16] Arriving at his views on the origin of Christ, he says that according to the heresiarch himself, Christ was brought forth by the Mother (i.e. Sophia); he came into being together with a shadow, after the Mother had ended up outside the Pleroma. Christ, however, cut himself loose from the shadow, left his mother and ascended to the Pleroma. The Mother then gave birth to another son, the Demiurge, and "together with him was emitted an archon on the left as well, in the same way as the falsely called Gnostics of whom we shall speak later."[17] Irenaeus is here offering a concrete piece of evidence to shore up his claim that Valentinus was inspired by the Gnostic *hairesis*. In fact, in chapter 30 he reports a system that contains a similar set of ideas. This system tells of a First Woman who was unable to contain all the light flowing to her from the two superior figures called the First Man/the Father and the Second Man/Son. She suffers a split. On the right side, she gave birth to Christ, and was taken up together with him into the aeon above. To the left, however, the light spilled over and became Sophia Prounikos, a male-female figure, who sank down into the lower regions and eventually gave birth to Yaldabaoth (1.30.2–5). It may be argued that there is not a complete fit in every detail between the two stories; however, for Irenaeus the similarity was evidently great enough to lend credence to his claim about Valentinus' sources.

To what extent Irenaeus' claim is justified, however, remains to be investigated. For that purpose, a comparative analysis of the information about the "Gnostics" given by Irenaeus in *Haer*. 1.29–31 and of what we know about Valentinian doctrine will be necessary. Specifically, the analysis will have to concentrate on the two systems described in chapters 29 and 30, where Irenaeus appears to be reporting original sources in some detail. The Valentinian system to which comparison can be made is known in several variants: from Irenaeus, from other patristic writers, and in the Nag Hammadi codices.[18] The question of the historical relationships between these two sets of documents is surprisingly

---

16 The attribution to Valentinus himself of the system reported in 1.11.1 is generally dismissed by contemporary scholarship (e.g. Markschies, *Valentinus*, 364–79; Thomassen, *Spiritual Seed*, 23–27). The summarising form of the report suggests that Irenaeus here depends on earlier, unidentified heresiological sources.
17 Συμπροβεβλῆσθαι δὲ αὐτῷ καὶ ἀριστερὸν ἄρχοντα ἐδογμάτισεν, ὁμοίως τοῖς ῥηθησομένοις ὑφ' ἡμῶν ψευδωνύμως γνωστικοῖς (1.11.1). See also below, p. 31.
18 More or less complete versions of the Valentinian system are found in Iren. *Haer*. 1.1–8, 1.11.1, 1.14–15; [Hipp.] *Haer*. 6.29.2–6.36; *Tri. Trac.* (NHC I,5); *Val. Exp.* (NHC XI,1). Less complete versions and fragments of other systems are attested by Epiphanius, *Pan*. 31.5–6, Clement of Alexandria's *Excerpts from Theodotus*, Iren. *Haer*. 1.11.2–1.12.

understudied, although it would be unfair to claim that it has been entirely ignored.[19]

Chapters 29 and 30 report two distinct treatises. The one used in chapter 29 is mainly a protological account, describing the generation and the architecture of the transcendent world. The figure of Barbelo here plays an important part. The account ends with a brief description of how the world creator, called the Protarchon, came into being, and of the subsequent creation of the world. In the treatise reported in chapter 30, the situation is the reverse. After a summary protology, the account concentrates on the creation and the structure of the cosmos, the creation of the human being, and the subsequently unfolding salvation history. In this treatise, the world creator is named Yaldabaoth and there is no mention of Barbelo.

Evidently, the two treatises represent two distinct mythological systems. Nevertheless, Irenaeus presents them as variant doctrines held by two groups that are both included in the common category of "the Gnostics".[20] I shall first discuss the system of chapter 29, which raises a few questions of its own.

4 Irenaeus, *Haer.* 1.29 and the *Apocryphon of John*

From the point of view of historical reconstruction, Irenaeus' testimony in chapter 29 is of special interest in that it is one of the rare instances where literary contact between a patristic source and a Nag Hammadi tractate can be detected with certainty. The tractate in question is the *Apocryphon of John*, a text that is preserved in three Coptic versions in the Nag Hammadi codices, while a fourth

---

[19] Deserving mention in particular are Anne McGuire's unpublished dissertation "Valentinus", and Alastair Logan's *Gnostic Truth*.

[20] The treatise of *Haer.* 1.29 is introduced by the words "Some of them maintain that ...", and that of 1.30 by "Others, however, say that ..." (cf. above, n. 15). As for the category to which both of these groups belong, Irenaeus begins chapter 29 by saying that he will now report the doctrines of "the great mass of Barbelo Gnostics (*multitudo gnosticorum Barbelo*)", which has sprung up "like mushrooms out of the ground". In their Sources Chrétiennes edition, Rousseau and Doutreleau argue that the word *Barbelo* cannot be part of the original text, but must be a later gloss (RD I/1, 296–99). I find their arguments quite persuasive: the figure of Barbelo appears only in 1.29 and not in the reports on the doctrines of the "others" who are said to belong to the same *multitudo*; moreover, whenever Irenaeus refers to "the Gnostics" in other parts of his work, Barbelo is never mentioned (cf. RD II/1, 350–54).

version is found in the famous Berlin Gnostic Codex (BG). A discussion of the position of Irenaeus' source on the trajectory leading from the "Gnostics" to the Valentinians must therefore also take into account the *Apocryphon of John* and its relationship to Irenaeus' report.

Judging by the number of preserved copies, the *Apocryphon of John* is a work that was widely circulated and much read. It exists in a short recension, which is preserved in the Berlin Codex and Nag Hammadi Codex III, each of which contains an independent Coptic translation of the text, as well as in a longer recension found in two nearly identical copies in Nag Hammadi Codices II and IV that evidently derive from the same Coptic translation, and probably were copied from the same *Vorlage*. Several other texts appear to have known and used this treatise.[21] The *Apocryphon* is regarded in current scholarship as a foundational document of Sethianism, a movement that is represented by a number of other Nag Hammadi tractates as well and whose internal coherence was first charted by Hans-Martin Schenke.[22] On the basis of the overlap between the "Gnostics" of Irenaeus and the "Sethians" of Nag Hammadi represented by the agreements between Iren. *Haer.* 1.29 and the *Apocryphon of John*, it has also become a widespread assumption that the two groups are more or less identical.[23] To evaluate this claim, however, the precise relationship between the *Apocryphon* and Iren. *Haer.* 1.29 requires closer examination.

The textual agreements between *Haer.* 1.29 and the *Apocryphon of John* were noted already by Carl Schmidt, who in 1896 had acquired the Berlin Codex for the Berlin Papyrus Collection. In 1907 he published an article in which he argued that the *Apocryphon* was in fact the source of Irenaeus' presentation of the Barbelo Gnostics in that chapter.[24] Today we must accept that that conclusion was inaccurate. The *Apocryphon of John* is, both in its short and its long version, a revelation dialogue. Here, Jesus appears after his resurrection to his disciple John and reveals to him the secrets about the transcendent god, the spiritual

---

21 *Allogenes* (NHC XI,*3*); the Audian treatise quoted by Theodore bar Koni; the Bala'izah fragment of an unknown Gnostic treatise; for these testimonies, see appendices 3, 5, and 6 in Waldstein and Wisse, *Apocryphon of John*. For the use of materials deriving from *Apocr. John* in the early Shiite *ghulāt* text *Umm al-kitāb*, see, most recently, Thomassen, "Melothesia".
22 See in particular Schenke, "Phenomenon". Schenke's various contributions to this field are assembled in *Der Same Seths*. Of fundamental importance is also Turner, *Sethian Gnosticism*.
23 E.g. Quispel, "Valentinian Gnosis"; Turner, *Sethian Gnosticism*, 57, 747; Brakke, *Gnostics*, 36–51. Tuomas Rasimus, on the other hand (*Paradise Reconsidered*), argues that "Sethianism" should be considered as a subgroup within, or deriving from, a more general category of "Classical Gnosticism", of which the systems of Iren. *Haer.* 1.29–30 are representatives.
24 Schmidt, "Irenäus und seine Quelle".

world, the creation of the cosmos, the entrapment of the spirit in human bodies, and the divine plan for salvation. Irenaeus, on the other hand, gives no indication that the text in his report had the form of a dialogue between Jesus and John – a piece of information we may well expect him to have mentioned if he knew of it.[25] Moreover, as was mentioned earlier, Irenaeus' source restricted itself to a protological account, whereas the *Apocryphon* continues with cosmology and salvation history.[26] Finally, careful comparison of Irenaeus' text with those of the four manuscripts of the *Apocryphon* reveals a number of differences that indicate that deliberate acts of revision were made when the document known to Irenaeus in *Haer.* 1.29 was transformed into the *Apocryphon.*[27] Perhaps the most significant modification is that the figure of Seth is given a central role in the mythology of the *Apocryphon,* whereas he is totally absent from *Haer.* 1.29.

The most likely scenario is therefore that Irenaeus in chapter 29 had access to a treatise that described the generation and the architecture of the spiritual world, in which the figure of Barbelo played a central role, and which ended with the story of Sophia and the Protarchon's entry on the stage. Later, this treatise was used as source material for a dialogue, in which a revised version of the text was put into the mouth of the resurrected Jesus as secret knowledge revealed to John. At the same time, this material was expanded to include materials on cosmology and soteriology taken from sources related to, but not identical with, the document used by Irenaeus in *Haer.* 1.30. A further feature of the revision consisted of the introduction of the figure of Seth as a key protagonist in the salvation historical narrative. In this way the *Apocryphon of John* became a "Sethian" text, which Irenaeus' source in *Haer.* 1.29 was not.[28]

This process has an instructive parallel in other parts of the Nag Hammadi library. The two texts *Eugnostos* (NHC III,*3* and V,*1*) and the *Wisdom of Jesus Christ* (NHC III,*1*; BG,*1*; P. Oxy. 1081) provide a tangible example of how such

---

[25] Logan, *Gnostic Truth,* 72–74.
[26] Cf. Schenke, "Das literarische Problem". The early discussions on this issue are reviewed by Logan, "Development," 3–12. Cf. also Logan, *Gnostic Truth,* 2, 42–43. Logan rightly points out that the myth told in 1.29 presupposes a larger salvation historical narrative. However, the treatise behind 1.29 may have restricted itself to telling only part of that narrative, just as is the case with *Eugnostos* and the Valentinian *Lehrbrief* of Epiphanius, *Pan.* 31.5–6. Regarding *Eug.*, Louis Painchaud has made the interesting suggestion that it forms a "diptych" with *Orig. World* (NHC II,*5*), which more or less starts where *Eug.* ends (Painchaud, "The Literary Contacts").
[27] See Logan, *Gnostic Truth,* 44–45. I hope to come back to this issue in more detail in another context.
[28] Cf. Logan, *Gnostic Truth,* 16–19.

rewriting could take place. *Eugnostos*, a treatise describing the architecture of the transcendent world, and containing no features that are obviously "Christian" in the sense familiar to us, was reused by the composer of *Wisdom of Jesus Christ*, in which it was set in the framework of a revelation dialogue as teaching materials for Jesus speaking to his disciples. Thus, the reframing of a theological-mythological treatise as a Christian dialogue is a more widely attested phenomenon. This kind of process obviously reflects a desire in some circles to bolster the Christian legitimacy of the doctrines contained in such treatises by recasting the texts as gospel-like apocrypha. This secondary apocryphisation of texts that were originally written as mythological treatises may be seen as a reflection of the general process of canonisation of scripture in the late second and third centuries. When the original treatises were written, their authors apparently did not feel the same need to authorise their teachings by employing the literary forms found in canonical scripture. They seem to have been written before apostolic canonicity became an issue among Christians. This is an important point, whose significance will become clearer towards the end of this lecture.

The Valentinians, as we know, wrote mythological treatises. In this respect, they continued using an already existing literary form, exemplified by the source reported in *Haer*. 1.29, a text that Irenaeus claims also served as a main source for the doctrine of Valentinus. If Irenaeus is right, that text is to be regarded as an *Urtext*, not only of the *Apocryphon of John*, but of the Valentinian system as well. It is now time to examine the doctrinal aspects of this relationship.

5 The mythological system of Irenaeus, *Haer.* 1.29

Irenaeus begins his presentation in *Haer*. 1.29 by focusing on the figure of Barbelo:

> Quidam enim eorum aeonem quendam numquam senescentem in uirginali spiritu subiciunt, quem Barbelon nominant: ubi esse Patrem quendam innominabilem dicunt. Voluisse autem hunc manifestare se ipsi Barbeloni. Ennoeam autem hanc stetisse in conscpectu eius et postulasse Prognosin. Cum prodiisset autem et Prognosis, his rursum petentibus prodiit Incorruptela, post deinde Vita aeterna.
> Some of them posit an unageing aeon dwelling in a virginal spirit that they call Barbelo. There was also an unnameable Father, they say; he wanted to reveal himself to that Barbelo. This Thought came forth, stood before him, and asked to be given Foreknowledge.

After Foreknowledge had appeared, the two of them asked and Incorruptibility came forth; after that, Eternal Life. (1.29.1)[29]

The highest deity, the unnameable Father, is not further described, except that in the course of the following narrative he is also called "the great Light" and "the Greatness".[30] Barbelo (whose name remains a mystery to scholarship) is the figure who sets the protological process in motion. We are told that the Father wished to reveal himself to Barbelo. But then we are told that the Father's wish manifested itself as his Thought, *Ennoia*, who stood before the Father as a distinct being and began to request favours of him – the three qualities of Foreknowledge, Incorruptibility and Eternal Life. The Father's self-revelation to Barbelo seems to be understood as a generative process by which Barbelo herself is brought into being as his Thought: the Father wills and thinks, and his Thought emerges as a distinct being.[31] Perhaps an earlier mythological theme of a primordial revelation to Barbelo has been overlaid by a more philosophical theory of divine self-reflection producing the first duality. I don't know.[32]

---

29 The paraphrase of Theodoret of Cyrus: ὑπέθεντο γὰρ αἰῶνά τινα ἀνώλεθρον ἐν παρθενικῷ διάγοντα πνεύματι, ὃ Βαρβηλὼθ ὀνομάζουσι, τὴν δὲ Βαρβηλὼθ αἰτῆσαι πρόγνωσιν παρ' αὐτοῦ. Προελθούσης δὲ ταύτης, εἶτ' αὖθις αἰτησάσης, προελήλυθεν Ἀφθαρσία, ἔπειτα αἰωνία Ζωή (*Haer. fab.* 1.13; RD I/1, 328).

30 The *Apocryphon of John*, on the other hand, contains a long section at the beginning of the narrative in which the supreme deity is described at length in the language of negative theology (BG 22:17–26:11; NHC II, 2:26–4:15 parr). This section can be assumed to be a later addition, not only because Irenaeus shows no sign of knowing it, but also because the name of the deity in the *Apocryphon*, the Invisible Spirit, never appears in Irenaeus' report. An analogous situation exists with the Valentinian treatises: the treatises reported by Irenaeus pass quickly over the Father himself in order to concentrate on the generation of the Pleroma. Only the *Tripartite Tractate* from Nag Hammadi starts out with an extensive description of the unknowable Father in the same style as the *Apocryphon of John* (NHC I, 51:8–54:35). Since *Tri. Trac.* appears to have been composed later than the Valentinian treatises reported by the church fathers, it seems as if the inclusion of this kind of material might be a secondary development in the redaction history of the Valentinian system texts. Extensive negative theologies appear to have been a later fashion.

31 Though *voluisse* 1.29.1 is probably a rendering of the Greek ἐννοηθῆναι (RD I/1, 302), the primordial divine act has a volitional as well as a cognitive aspect. *Thelema* will later in the narrative be introduced as an independent hypostasis, distinct from *Ennoia*.

32 All the entities and qualities produced by the Father will have roles to play in the later narrative by combining into generative pairs ("syzygies"); only Barbelo is left out from this activity. This suggests that she is in fact identified with Thought, which there appears as the partner of Logos, and that the name Barbelo, which is redundant from the point of view of the internal logic of the narrative, is a remnant of an earlier mythology.

Having been granted the three attributes she requested, Barbelo/Ennoia is filled with joy and gazes into the Father's Greatness. By that act, she gives birth to a third figure called the Light, who is similar to the great light of the Father. In order to make the offspring perfect, the Father anoints it and it becomes Χριστός.[33] In philosophical terms, we may here detect a process of emanation comprised of three stages, similar to what we find in the Platonist tradition: an initial outward movement producing a second being, followed by the turning of this entity towards its source, and finally, as a result, the consolidation of the emanated entity by means of an illumination received from the source.[34]

The Light-Christos[35] asks to be given two attributes: Intellect (*nous*) and *logos*. This request having been granted, we are then told that all the elements which have so far been put into play form a total of four conceptual pairs – *syzygoi* – that are instrumental in the further process of generation: Ennoia and Logos pair up to produce a figure called Autogenes, the Self-generated one; Incorruptibility and Christos bring forth four luminaries (Armogenes, Raguhel, David, Eleleth)[36] that attend to Autogenes; Eternal Life and Will produce four mental faculties (*charis, thelesis, synesis,* and *phronesis*) that are to assist the four luminaries. The fourth pair, Nous and Prognosis, is, strangely, not credited with any particular task in the further process of generation as reported by Irenaeus (1.29.2).

---

33 *In quibus gloriantem Barbelon et prospicientem in Magnitudinem et conceptu delectatam in hanc, generasse simile ei Lumen. Hanc initium et luminationis et generationis omnium dicunt. Et uidentem Patrem Lumen hoc, unxisse illud sua benignitate, ut perfectum fieret: hunc autem dicunt esse Christum* (1.29.1). Theodoret: Εὐφρανθεῖσαν δὲ τὴν Βαρβηλὼθ ἐνκύμονα γενέσθαι καὶ ἀποτεκεῖν τὸ Φῶς. Τοῦτό φασι τῇ τοῦ Πατρὸς χρισθὲν τελειότητι ὀνομασθῆναι Χριστόν.
34 For Platonism, cf. in particular Krämer, *Geistmetaphysik*, 312–37 and Halfwassen, *Spuren*, 146–48, 161–64, who argue that the πρόοδος-ἐπιστροπή-doctrine elaborated in later Platonism may be traced back to the Old Academy (Speusippus). The Gnostic and Valentinian evidence suggests that the doctrine was around and exerted influence in the first half of the second century, and probably earlier as well. Pursuing the Platonist connections in detail lies, however, beyond the scope of this lecture.
35 In the following, the name "Christos" will be used for this specifically Gnostic figure, which belongs to a context and an age where the "Christ" of traditional Christian theology is still unknown.
36 In the *Apocryphon of John,* the names of the four luminaries are Harmozel, Oroiael, Daueithe, and Eleleth. The different forms of the two first names may be due to corruption in the transmission of Irenaeus' text and constitute a rather uncertain basis on which to build hypothesis about the literary relationship between the *Apocryphon* and *Haer.* 1.29, as Antti Marjanen attempts ("The *Apocryphon of John,*" 242).

Furthermore, we are told that Autogenes, with Aletheia, Truth, as his partner, emits the Perfect Human Being, Adamas. He possesses Perfect Knowledge as his partner, and is endowed with invincible power given directly by Barbelo herself. Adamas is said, somewhat enigmatically, to have given birth to a "tree" (1.29.3).

Finally, the Holy Spirit, also named Sophia Prounikos,[37] is emitted by "the first angel who stands by the Monogenes".[38] Lacking a partner, she produces an offspring in ignorance and presumption (*ignorantia et audacia*); this is the Protarchon, who will go on to create the world and make himself its master.

---

37 The precise meaning implied by the name Προύνικος is hard to pin down. The basic sense of the noun is that of a "porter", a servant, hired or employed, who transports something from one place to another. Motion seems to be an integral part of the concept. But προύνικοι could also be portrayed as being impetuous and hard to control, for instance in comedy; the word therefore connotes emotional as well as physical motility. In the Gnostic context, the term seems to have acquired a technical significance as a description of the outward movement represented by Sophia, which creates division and plurality, and also, sometimes, her impulsivity. The frequent translation of the word in this context as "lewd", should in any case be avoided; no moral judgment is involved, I think, in calling Sophia προύνικος. For an excellent study of the term, see Pasquier, "Prouneikos".

38 *Deinde ex primo Angelo qui adstat Monogeni emissum dicunt Spiritum sanctum, quem et Sophiam et Prunicum uocant* (1.29.4).

The account may be schematically represented as follows:

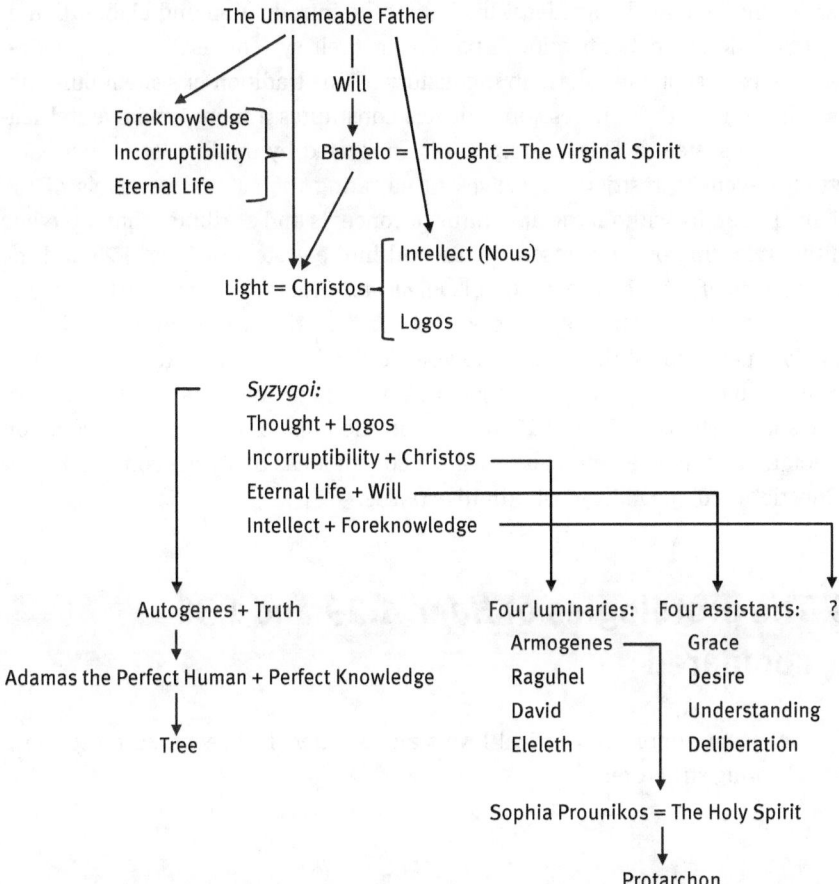

It is fairly evident that the document reported by Irenaeus is itself a composite work and the product of a perhaps extensive process of rewriting, compilation and experimentation. For instance, the final section that tells the story of Sophia introduces vocabulary that has not been used in the previous account: the luminaries are now "angels", and Christos is referred to as the Monogenes. Thus, a different source may here be suspected. Moreover, the protology itself appears to have been constructed on the basis of two distinct sets of materials. On the one hand, it has a grid that consists of a vertical structure with a succession of distinct levels. On the other hand, it introduces a certain number of concepts, qualities and attributes that are instrumental in moving from one level to the next and ultimately form generative pairs. The protological process progresses through the interaction of these two sets of respectively static and dynamic components. I consider it likely that the introduction and elaboration of the dynamic components and, in particular, their systematisation as syzygies, represents a secondary phase in the history of this tradition of system building, and that the vertical succession of levels constitutes a more fundamental feature of the system.[39] This assumption is supported by the fact that other early systems seem to restrict themselves to narrating the successive levels of the divine hierarchy without the apparatus of concepts and attributes that intervene in the unfolding of the transcendent world in the system of *Haer.* 1.29 and the *Apocryphon of John*. A case in point is *Eugnostos*. Another instance is the second system attributed by Irenaeus to the "Gnostics", in 1.30, whose protology is also simply an account of the levels following vertically after the paternal first principle.[40] I shall now proceed to a comparison of the divine hierarchies in the two "Gnostic" systems of *Haer.* 1.29 and 1.30 in the hope of finding some common denominators that can guide us toward a core of ideas that were constitutive for "Gnostic" theology in its most primitive phase.

6 The protologies of *Haer.* 1.29 and 1.30 compared

If we concentrate on the vertical levels alone, *Haer.* 1.29 seems to presuppose the following structure:

---

39 In particular the three attributes requested by Barbelo and the two requested by Christos seem to be introduced primarily in order to provide members for the four syzygies who will play an active part in the subsequent generative process. The Thought and the Will, on the other hand, are concepts that appear in several comparable protological texts and probably therefore represent a more primitive layer of the system.
40 For a schematic comparison of the protologies of *Eug.* and Iren. *Haer.* 1.30, cf. Rasimus, *Paradise Reconsidered*, 45–47.

The protologies of Haer. 1.29 and 1.30 compared — 19

The Unnameable Father = The Great Light
↓
Barbelo = Ennoia = The Virginal Spirit
↓
Light = Christos
↓
The Self-generated One (Autogenes)
↓
Adamas = The Perfect Man
↓
Tree = Knowledge

The treatise used by Irenaeus in 1.30, on the other hand, presents the following account:

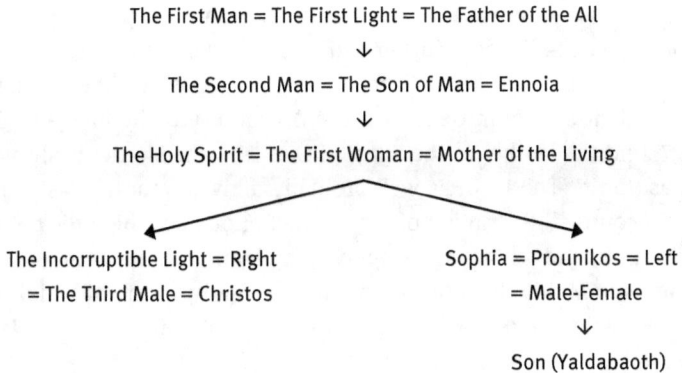

In the latter account, the Father of the All is himself called the First Man. He brings forth a Second Man as his Thought. Then there is a First Woman, also called the Holy Spirit and the Mother of the Living. We are not told how she came into being; it is only said that she is *sub his*, i.e. below the two male figures. The following events have already been referred to above (p. 9): The First Woman receives the light of the Father and the Son, but it is so overwhelming that she is unable to contain all of it. In consequence, she gives birth to Christos the Light on the one hand – specifically on the right-hand side – while on the left-hand side some of the light spills over and becomes Sophia Prounikos, whose passions will set in motion the rest of the story: the birth of Yaldabaoth and the creation of the material world.

This protology clearly uses many of the same basic elements as the one in 1.29. Most notable is the idea of a Primordial Man, but the divine Thought (Ennoia), a mother figure and Christos are also parts of the mythological skeleton around which both systems are built. So too are the notions of Light and Spirit; the Light being associated especially with the Father and Christos, and the Spirit with the mother figure. However, these elements are combined differently in the two systems. This situation invites hypotheses regarding their common origin. It seems plausible, for instance, that behind both of them lies a theory of a primordial, unknowable and divine Father, characterised as Light, who by an act of mental self-reflection produces a second entity, his personified *ennoia*. In 1.29 the Ennoia is understood as a female figure: she is Barbelo, the Virginal Spirit, who subsequently becomes the mother of Christos. In contrast, in 1.30, the Ennoia is a male Anthropos. Which of these versions is the more original one, is open for debate. It may be that the male Anthropos version was there first, and that the alternative identification of the Ennoia with a mother figure happened as a result of a wish to give Christos a prominent place in the structure. In that way, the Father-Mother-Child model came to replace the God-Primordial Man model. Be that as it may, the Anthropos and the Mother both seem to have their source in Genesis 1: the Anthropos as the image of God in Gen 1:26–27, and the Mother as the Spirit of Gen 1:2 – the Mother is always also conceived as Spirit. (The Light as well probably derives from the first verses of Genesis 1.) In contrast, the notion of the divine Ennoia, by which the deity contemplates himself, and which is presupposed by both versions, is more likely to have its origins in Middle Platonism – more specifically a form of Middle Platonism that has assimilated the Aristotelian concept of νοῦς with the Platonist theory of Forms.

It is evident, at any rate, that those who constructed these systems wanted to have it both ways: they were working hard to harmonise the two models, trying to include in some way both the primordial Anthropos and the primordial Mother. A further example of this concern is that the *Apocryphon of John* declares Barbelo to be the πρῶτος ἄνθρωπος, making her androgynous in the process: she is Mother, Spirit and First Man in one person.[41] That identification is not made in Irenaeus 1.29; the author of the *Apocryphon* apparently felt a need to improve upon his source on this point. The treatise of 1.29, whose focus is on Barbelo as Thought and Mother, had, however, already tried to incorporate the Primordial Anthropos using another device. It had introduced the figure of the Autogenes, the Self-generated One, at a lower level in the hierarchy. As seen

---

41 BG 27:19–20, 29:9–10; NHC II, 5:7, 6:3–4.

above, he was generated by the syzygy Ennoia and Logos after Christos had come into being. The Autogenes, in turn, emits Adamas, the Perfect Human Being; being the model of Adamas, Autogenes is to be regarded as a Primordial Anthropos figure. Roelof van den Broek has made the cogent observation that the Autogenes figure is named and described in ways which suggest that he originally belonged in a more exalted context.[42] That is to say, Autogenes was probably imported into the system of 1.29 from a source no longer known to us, where he was conceived as a Primordial Anthropos occupying the second rank in the hierarchy, as the primary manifestation of the supreme deity. The *Apocryphon of John*, however, had no more use for Autogenes as a distinct figure, having identified Barbelo with the Primordial Anthropos. Instead, it assimilated Autogenes with Christos the Light, understanding Autogenes as just another name for Christos, and contrived a different genealogy for Adamas.

7 The Valentinian reception of Gnostic protology

Ennoia – the Thought

Now let us turn to the Valentinians, who Irenaeus says created their systems on the basis of the "Gnostic" doctrine described in his chapters 29 and 30. The first thing to be observed is that the Valentinians took over the Ennoia concept of the Gnostics as a starting point in their systems. For example, the Valentinian model system presented by Irenaeus states that, together with the First Father (Προπάτωρ, Προαρχή, Βυθός), Thought, Ennoia also existed at the beginning. The text adds that she is also called Grace (Χάρις) and Silence (Σιγή).[43] Similar formulations with the same lists of names are found in other sources.[44] "Those who speak truly, however, call her Silence," the Valentinian *Lehrbrief* in Epiphanius declares. Thus, these Valentinians knew and adopted the female

---

[42] Van den Broek, "Autogenes and Adamas". Autogenes stands in attendance to the supreme deity (*repraesentationem magni Luminis* 1.29.2 corresponds to ⲉⲅⲛⲁ]ⲣⲁⲥⲧⲁⲥⲓⲥ in *Apocr. John* NHC III, 11:5), he is greatly honoured and is given power over all things. Van den Broek persuasively argues that Ps 8:4–6 is the original source of these ideas. The anthropology of that psalm is based, of course, on Near Eastern conceptions of sacred kingship: the human creature is, like the king, the deputy of the deity.
[43] συνυπάρχειν δ' αὐτῷ καὶ Ἔννοιαν, ἣν δὴ καὶ Χάριν, καὶ Σιγὴν ὀνομάζουσι, *Haer.* 1.1.1.
[44] Cf. The Valentinian *Lehrbrief* in Epiph. *Pan.* 31.5.4; *Tri. Trac.* 57:3–8.

Ennoia figure of the Gnostics of Irenaeus 1.29, but preferred to name her Silence.[45]

By contrast, the *Tripartite Tractate* from Nag Hammadi prefers a masculine version, and identifies the Father's Thought with the Son:

> By knowing himself in himself the Father bore him without generation, so that he exists by the Father having him as a thought – that is, his thought about himself ... This is what in truth is meant by "Silence," or "Wisdom," or "Grace", as the latter is also rightly called. (56:33–57:8)

Thus, the *Tripartite Tractate* is in line with Irenaeus 1.30 rather than with 1.29 on this point. The similarity is increased by the fact that the *Tripartite Tractate* also explicitly describes the Son as a Primordial Anthropos: "... he alone is truly the Father's first human being" (66:10–12). In this capacity, the text explains, the Son reveals the unknowable and unnameable Father; he bears all the Father's names and thereby gives birth to the All, that is, to the totality of individual aeons. He is the form of that which is without form, the body of the incorporeal, the face, *prosopon,* of the invisible. As the First Human, the Son is, in other words, the manifested image of the Father.

With regard to the female Sige-Ennoia of the Valentinian systems reported by the church fathers, it should be noted that she is generally a much less active figure than the Barbelo of Irenaeus 1.29[46] – a change that may, in fact, be reflected in her renaming as Silence. What we have in these systems is actually an elaboration of the Father-Ennoia concept into a tetrad of terms: The Father and his Ennoia, renamed Forefather/Bythos and Silence respectively, give birth to the Monogenes as their son together with Truth and it is the Monogenes, who is also named Mind (*nous*) and Father, who becomes the main agent in the subsequent unfolding of the Pleroma. Ennoia-Sige is no longer a mother figure giving birth to Christos as in the pre-Valentinian systems. In fact, the Valentinian system reported in [Hippolytus], *Haer.* 6.29–30 has eliminated her completely. It may therefore be said that, on the whole, the Valentinians replaced the female Ennoia, the Barbelo of Irenaeus 1.29 and the *Apocryphon of John*, with the male Son.

---

[45] Σιγή is also the name used in the system attributed to Valentinus in Iren. *Haer.* 1.11.1 and in the *Valentinian Exposition* of NHC XI. *Exc. Theod.* 6–7:3 rephrases Ἔννοια as Ἐνθύμησις, Iren. *Haer.* 1.8.5 prefers Χάρις, [Hipp.] *Haer.* 6.29 attributes no partner at all to the Father.

[46] An exception to this is the Valentinian *Lehrbrief*, in which the Ennoia-Sige plays an unusually active role in the manifestation of the Pleroma (Epiph. *Pan.* 31.5.3). For more on this text, see the interesting study by Chiapparini, *Il divino senza veli.*

The Primordial Anthropos

From the Son, also named "Father", the Valentinian Pleroma spreads out into a multitude of aeons. In its most widely attested form that Pleroma is composed of 30 aeons, each of which has an individual name. The Monogenes Son, together with his *syzygos* Truth, generates another couple, Logos and Life, who in turn give birth to Anthropos and Ecclesia. Together with the Forefather and Sige all these aeons constitute the primary Ogdoad. Logos and Life then emit 10 aeons in pairs, and Anthropos and Ecclesia 12 aeons, the last of which is the ill-fated Sophia. I shall not dwell on the details here. It is more important to note that the *Tripartite Tractate* omits all the names and the numbers of the aeons and states that the Son himself encompasses and operates within all the individual aeons. In this way they can all be said to be manifestations of himself, as he spreads out from oneness to multiplicity. The Son is himself an image of the hidden Father; as such he is the primordial human figure, and this Primordial Anthropos is a corporate entity consisting of a multitude of spiritual beings (*Tri. Trac.* 62:33–67:34).

It was primarily by means of the figure of the Son, I would suggest, that the Valentinians took over and elaborated on the idea of a First Man, the image of God, which had earlier been developed in the circles that Irenaeus calls "the Gnostic sect." However, they also seem to have added a significant dimension to this idea in that they emphasised the collective character of the Primordial Anthropos. This dimension is also indicated by the pairing of the aeon Anthropos with Ecclesia in the systems that apply the theory of the primary Ogdoad. (Of course, each of the single aeons is to be understood as an aspect of the Son himself, who encompasses them all.) The impetus for this addition most probably came from Pauline Christo-ecclesiology: the Valentinians inherited the concept of a Primordial Anthropos from the Gnostics and fused it with the idea of the Church as the body of Christ found in the letters of Paul. This revision of the concept is also an indication of the Valentinians' stronger consciousness of being an *ekklesia* compared to their Gnostic predecessors.

In order to understand the full significance of the concept of the First Man in Valentinianism, it is necessary to recapitulate briefly the Valentinian version of the myth of Sophia, in which the creation of earthly human beings in the image of the pleromatic archetype is an essential feature.

According to the standard narrative of the Valentinian systems, Sophia is the youngest of all the aeons. She is filled with a desire to know the unknown Father; since that knowledge is unattainable for a single aeon, her desire becomes an uncontrollable passion that leads her into the infinite void. Her progress is arrested, however, by an entity called the Boundary (Ὅρος), which cuts her in two. Her spiritual part is returned to the Pleroma inside the Boundary, while her passion is left on the outside. This passion is usually named Sophia as well, though Irenaeus' main Valentinian source invented the special name Achamoth so as to distinguish the fallen aeon from her redeemed mother. She becomes desperate, repents and prays for help. The aeons are filled with compassion for their lost sister, and collectively bring forth the Saviour to redeem her. He is sent out together with an entourage of angels. In this way he is a manifestation of the Pleroma in its unity as well as its diversity. He appears to Sophia, and in response to this vision, she emits a spiritual seed, which comes into being as images of the host of angels. Next, Sophia brings forth a being whose nature is soul, derived from her sentiment of repentance. He is the Demiurge, and his task will be to create the cosmos and, after that, the human being, both of these being composed of matter and soul. The Saviour and Sophia control all the Demiurge's actions, though he is not aware of it. Their plan is to sow the spiritual seed into the humans created by the Demiurge, so that they will one day be able to learn about the higher, spiritual world and go there. That event takes place when the Saviour comes down into the world as Jesus, awakens the hidden spirit in humans, and initiates the ritual of redemption. This ritual (actually a form of baptism) enables the spiritual seed to be united with their angelic counterparts. This unification is what is called "the bridal chamber."

This brief summary of the narrative should make clear the relationship between humans on earth and the First Human. Through the spirit sown in them, earthly humans are images of the angels, who themselves are manifestations of the multiple aeons of the Pleroma. The aeons in turn are collectively the members of the Primordial Anthropos, who himself is the revealed image of the hidden deity. Spiritual humans, who collectively form the Church, are thus an earthly representation, through the intermediary of the Saviour and his angels, of the Pleroma, which is co-extensive with the corporative Primordial Anthropos:

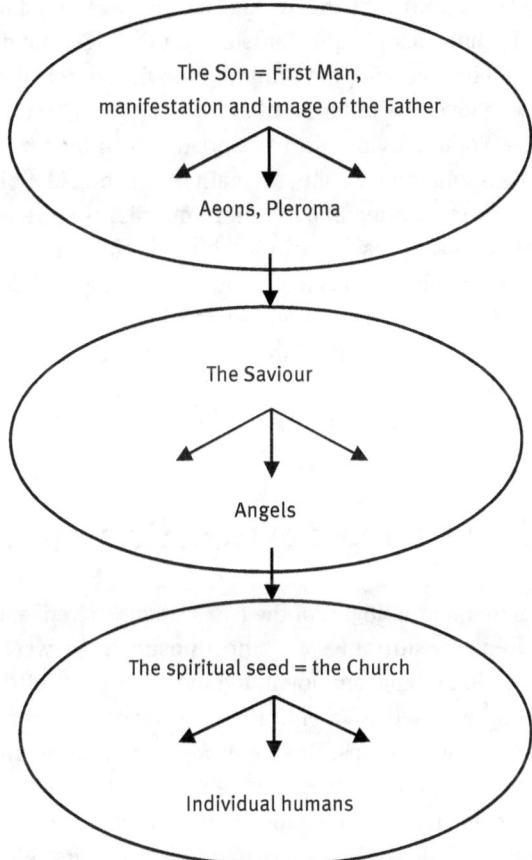

The fundamental importance in the Valentinian system of the Primordial Anthropos concept, inherited from Irenaeus' "Gnostics", is thus beyond doubt.

Sophia and Christos

A further point of correspondence between the Valentinian systems and those of Irenaeus 1.29 and 1.30 exists in the figures of Sophia and Christos. In the treatise reported in chapter 29, as mentioned, Barbelo emerges from the unnameable Father, stands before him, receives light, and then gives birth to Christos. Sophia and her passion enter the story at a much later stage. In the treatise in chapter 30, on the other hand, the trouble starts much earlier, with the First Woman. Here, we are told that the Woman is unable to contain all the light streaming on her; she gives birth to Christos "on the right-hand side", but the light spills over and becomes Sophia Prounikos on the left (cf. above p. 9, 19).

As mentioned above, the latter motif has a close parallel in some Valentinian texts that have Sophia giving birth to Christos, who then hastens back into the Pleroma while Sophia herself must remain on the outside.[47] In other Valentinian versions, also mentioned above, the primordial rupture is depicted as a split within Sophia herself, resulting in a higher Sophia who is restored to the Pleroma and a lower Sophia who is left below.[48] For the generation of Christos a different solution is found.[49] The latter version in my view represents a later development within Valentinianism; the version that understands the rupture as a separation of Christos from his mother Sophia, in a way similar to the account in Irenaeus 1.30, is likely to be the more primitive one.[50]

8 The underlying logic of Gnostic protology

Now let us return to the protologies of the two systems in Irenaeus 1.29 and 1.30, both of which Irenaeus attributes to "the Gnostics". As we have seen, the protologies of the two systems employ much the same repertoire of terms, most of which was adopted by the Valentinians. However, this repertoire is used differently in the various systems. How may we explain these differences? Laying the elements of vocabulary out on the table, like the pieces of a puzzle, we have a set of names that for the most part have female connotations: the Thought, the Spirit, Wisdom, the Mother, and also the First Woman. Male figures are the Father, the First Man, and Christos. The Thought is sometimes considered to be male and identified with the First Man figure.[51]

---

[47] Cf. above, p. 9. Iren. *Haer.* 1.11.1; *Exc. Theod.* 23.2, 32–33; *Val. Exp.* 33. Cf. Thomassen, *Spiritual Seed*, 251–57.
[48] Iren. *Haer.* 1.2.2; [Hipp.] *Haer.* 6.30.7; *Exc. Theod.* 45.2; Thomassen, *Spiritual Seed*, 257–62.
[49] He is brought forth, together with the Holy Spirit, by the Monogenes in order to consolidate the Pleroma after the restoration of the higher Sophia (Iren. *Haer.* 1.2.5, etc.).
[50] I argue for this more extensively in "Relative Chronology," 20–24.
[51] See the comments on the *Tripartite Tractate* above. In Irenaeus 1.30, the Thought is actually the Second Man/the Son of Man and the First Man is the Father himself; this construction, however, clearly presupposes the idea that the Second Man is the image of the deity and thus

When understood as a female figure, the Thought, Ennoia, is generally kept distinct from the passionate and imperfect Wisdom. In contrast, Spirit and Mother are names that may be used both for Wisdom and for the exalted Ennoia. The First Woman of Irenaeus 1.30 is an ambiguous figure that seems to combine traits of both the Ennoia and the Sophia figures of other systems. Ambiguity is also present in the figure of Christos, who may be associated with passion through his connection with Sophia, but also with liberation from passion through his separation from her.

It has sometimes been suggested that the two types of females both go back to single figure, the Wisdom that accompanied God when he created the world, according to the biblical books of Proverbs and the Wisdom of Solomon, and that this figure was at one point split into a higher and a lower version.[52] This is not an implausible suggestion, though we lack solid historical evidence – some kind of "missing link" – that may reveal how the exalted biblical Wisdom figure could become the "fallen" Sophia of the Gnostics.[53]

On the basis of the evidence given by the systems we have been discussing here, however, I think a somewhat more pertinent observation can be made: a tendency toward reduplication seems to be intrinsic to the logic of the systems themselves. As mentioned above, the protologies of Irenaeus 1.29 and the *Apocryphon of John* make use of a model that distinguishes three phases in the process of manifestation: the procession of the Thought-Barbelo from the Father, her turning towards the source in glorification, and consolidation of the process through the generation of Christos the Light.[54] The system of 1.30 presents a different version. There, we are told that the First Woman was unable to contain all the light streaming from the Father/the First Man and his Son. She did indeed give birth to Christos, but some of the light spilled over and became Sophia Prounikos. Thus, it may be thought that the figure of Barbelo-the Holy Spirit of 1.29 has been split into the two figures of the First Female and Sophia Prounikos in 1.30.

---

represents the Primordial Anthropos in his manifested form. In the *Apocryphon of John*, Barbelo is identified with the First Man and described as androgynous (cf. above, p. 20).

52 I am thinking in particular of the important contribution by Stead, "Valentinian Myth."
53 Cf. MacRae, "Jewish Background."
54 The fact that this lecture is being given in Jena and Berlin, impels me to note that the structure in question bears an uncanny resemblance to central ideas in German idealism: Entäußerung, Gegenständlichkeit, Aufhebung. There probably is in fact a historical connection here, through the intermediary of later Platonism, as is suggested by the work of Krämer and Halfwassen (see above, n. 34).

It is fairly obvious that the underlying rationale for this notion of a split is a genuine theo-ontological dilemma: if the deity is essentially infinite, how can he manifest himself in distinctly perceivable form without his self-manifestation becoming an infinitely continuous process? The system of 1.29 seems simply to assert that the divine self-manifestation is complete through the illumination of Barbelo and her giving birth to Christos. There is no direct connection between Barbelo and Sophia Prounikos, who appears much later in the story. In 1.30, on the other hand, ambivalence about the manifestation process is evident already at the initial stages of the protology. It first appears in the distinction made between the Son/Second Man as the Ennoia on the one hand and the First Woman as the Holy Spirit on the other, a distinction that already suggests a degree of imperfection in the First Woman. Secondly, the ambivalence continues in the account of the direct generation by the First Woman of Prounikos, who is the personification of the First Woman's imperfection: the inability of the First Woman to receive all of the divine light.

Furthermore, the narratives about the "fall" and eventual restoration of Sophia can be seen to mirror in significant ways the primary protological model of procession, turning, and ultimate consolidation. The movement of procession – represented variously by the Thought, Barbelo, the Son, or the First Woman – corresponds in the case of Sophia with her "extension" towards infinity, her sinking downwards, and her inability to reproduce an authentic image of the transcendent deity (*extendebatur et prospiciebat ad inferiores partes ... generauit opus in quo erat ignorantia et audacia*, 1.29.4; ἐκτεινόμενον ἀεὶ ἐπὶ τὸ πρόσθεν, 1.2.2 [Valentinians]; *a patribus decidisse deorsum*, 1.30.3). In a second movement, she repents, turns back, and prays for help (*contristata refugit et in altiora secessit*, 1.29.4; *resipisse aliquando et conatam esse fugere aquas et ascendere ad matrem*, 1.30.3; *contristatam inuocasse in adiutorium matrem*, 1.30.12; ἐπισυμβεβηκέναι δ' αὐτῇ καὶ ἑτέραν διάθεσιν, τὴν τῆς ἐπιστροφῆς ἐπὶ τὸν ζωοποιήσαντα, 1.4.1 end; ἐπὶ ἱκεσίαν τραπῆναι τοῦ καταλιπόντος αὐτὴν φωτός, 1.4.5 [Valentinians][55]). Finally, and in response to her entreaties, Christos is sent down to Sophia, and she is united with her brother: *et descendentem Christum in hunc mundum, induisse primum sororem suam Sophiam, et exsultasse utrosque refrigerantes super inuicem*, 1.30.12. In this way, the original split between Chris-

---

[55] The movement of turning around, described as ἐπιστροφή and μετάνοια, is an essential feature of the Valentinian Sophia narrative: Iren. *Haer.* 1.2.2, 3 (the theme appears in connection with the "higher" Sophia as well as with Achamoth in 1.4.1 etc.); [Hipp.] *Haer.* 6.32.3, 6; *Tri. Trac.* 81:20–26; *Exp. Val.* 34:23. The supplication for help (βοήθεια) is also a standard feature of this movement (cf. [Hipp.] *Haer.* 6.32.3, 5.

tos and Sophia Prounikos, caused by the First Woman's inability to absorb all the light of the first two Males, is healed and the divine self-manifestation is at long last successful.

To be sure, the ultimate unification takes place only after a very long detour, during which Sophia gives birth to the Creator-Ruler, the latter organises the physical universe, and the human being is created as the vehicle for retrieving the remainder of the light that went astray with Sophia Prounikos. This succession of events is construed somewhat differently in the Gnostic system of Irenaeus, *Haer.* 1.30, in the various Valentinian systems, in the *Apocryphon of John,* and in other "Sethian" systems. A detailed analysis of these variations must be dispensed with in the present context. The main points to which I want to draw attention here, are two. First, the account in Irenaeus 1.30 suggests that the roots of the story of the "fall" of Sophia are to be sought in the theoretical dilemmas posed by the concept of divine self-manifestation as such. In that account, Sophia Prounikos is generated because the process of divine exteriorisation as First Man, Thought, and Holy Spirit is not immediately stabilised by the exteriorised entities turning towards their source and receiving illumination. Instead, stabilisation is deferred to a second cycle of procession, conversion, and reunification (within which are embedded still further and structurally analogous processes involving the residue of light deriving from Sophia Prounikos). This duplication into two (or even more) successive cycles may be seen as an expression of the inherent difficulty in explaining the initial moment of manifestation of infinite divinity: the two horns of this dilemma are represented by the First Woman, on the one hand, producing Christos and restoration, and Sophia Prounikos, on the other, producing ignorance and Yaldabaoth.

The second point to be stressed is that the figure of Christos occupies a central position in all these accounts. His essential role seems to be that of consolidating the manifestation process. In Irenaeus 1.29, as later in the *Apocryphon of John,* the generation of Christos represents the final moment of the tripartite process: after Barbelo has turned towards the Father as the source of her being, she is illuminated by him and gives birth to Christos, who is like the Father and is subsequently made perfect by him through an act of 'anointing'. In 1.30, on the other hand, Christos is brought forth in a pair with Sophia Prounikos. There, the illumination of the First Woman is incomplete; a portion of the primordial light goes astray with Sophia and is not restored to the incorruptible aeon until Sophia is united with Christos at the end of the cosmic salvation history. In this account as well, Christos is the figure who brings about the consolidation of the divine manifestation process, but in this case the consolidation takes place only after a lengthy diversion through the realms of ignorance and matter.

It would appear that the inherent ambivalence regarding the manifestation of divine infinity has given rise to two distinct conceptions of this process. On the one hand, there is what may be described as a model of *pre-established consolidation*. This model is represented by the source of Irenaeus 1.29, where the manifestation process is completed with the generation and anointing of Christos, and where the "fall" of Sophia is attributed to arbitrary caprice on the part of Sophia herself. In contrast, the system of Irenaeus 1.30 presents a model of *deferred consolidation*: in this model, the divine self-manifestation is not accomplished until Sophia is eventually united with Christos. In the first model the protology and the story of fall and redemption are treated as two discrete series of events, whereas in the second model the entire salvation history that unfolds in the physical cosmos is embedded in an overarching protological concept.

Turning to the Valentinian systems, we observe a similar situation.[56] The systems reported by Irenaeus (*Haer.* 1.1–8) and Hippolytus (*Haer.* 6.29–36) align themselves with the model of pre-established consolidation. In these texts, Sophia is restored to the Pleroma once her *enthymesis*, her misguided desire, has been eliminated. At the same time, the Monogenes (Son) and Truth bring forth Christos, in a pair with the Holy Spirit, for the task of consolidating the Pleroma.[57] By these acts, the protological process is consummated. In the *Tripartite Tractate*, on the other hand, the fall of the last aeon (here called "the Logos") is understood as a continuation of the unfolding of the Pleroma. The fall was caused by the constitutional inability of a single aeon to perceive the inconceivable and ineffable Father (NHC I, 75:17–76:23), and it was a necessity foreseen by the Father himself (76:23–77:11). That necessity consists in the fact that the ensuing creation of the physical cosmos forms part of a salvation economy (*oikonomia*) by which not only the Logos himself and his offspring, the spiritual seed, but even the aeons of the Pleroma will ultimately attain redemption.[58] This text, then, employs the model of deferred consolidation. That model can also be detected in the *Gospel of Truth*.[59]

A further important point to consider is the fact that the figure of Christos appears to occupy a different position in each of the two models. In the deferred

---

56 For the following, see Thomassen, *Spiritual Seed*, 182–84, 260–61, 313–14.
57 εἰς πῆξιν καὶ στηριγμὸν τοῦ πληρώματος, Iren. *Haer.* 1.2.5. Cf. Hipp. *Haer.* 6.31.2–5 (with a divergent division of labour between Christos and the Cross).
58 See 77:6–11, and 124:25–32, 126:9–15. Specifically, the redemption takes place through the ritual of baptism (127:25–28, and the following text); cf. Thomassen, *Spiritual Seed*, 180–85.
59 Thomassen, *Spiritual Seed*, ch. 17.

consolidation model of Irenaeus 1.30, Christos is closely associated with Sophia: he is the son of the First Woman and the brother of Sophia. In the model of preestablished consolidation represented by Irenaeus 1.29, on the other hand, Christos is brought forth by Barbelo interacting with the Unnameable Father. Here, Christos has nothing to do with Sophia, but comes into being to consolidate the primordial manifestation process. Similarly, in the Valentinian versions of the preestablished consolidation model, Christos is produced by the Monogenes to perfect the Pleroma after the excision of Sophia's *enthymesis*. As already mentioned, however, some Valentinian versions of the myth exist that associate Christos closely with Sophia. According to the system attributed to "Valentinus" in Irenaeus 1.11.1, "Christ ... was born, together with a certain shadow by the Mother after she had ended up outside .... And he, being male, cut away the shadow from himself and hastened back into the Pleroma. But the Mother, left alone with the shadow and emptied of her spiritual substance, brought forth another son, and this is the Demiurge ...." This motif is also attested in the *Excerpts from Theodotus* (23.2, 32–33) and probably in *A Valentinian Exposition* (NHC XI, 33:20–37).[60] Unlike the account in Irenaeus 1.30, Christos in these texts is not Sophia's brother, but her son. That difference is not of decisive importance, however. The basic motif in both texts is that of the split between Christos and Sophia: Christos ascends back into the Pleroma, Sophia is left below.

If the pattern of a correlation between each of the two consolidation models and a particular theory regarding the generation of Christos were to hold for the Valentinian as well as the Gnostic evidence, we would expect the Valentinian sources that describe Christos as the son of Sophia also to display the model of deferred consolidation. Unfortunately, the evidence is not transparent enough to allow decisive confirmation of that prediction. The relevant passages in Irenaeus 11.1 and *Exc.* 23, 32–33 lack a wider context that would allow us to perceive the overall structure of the systems to which they belong, and *Val. Exp.* is too fragmentarily preserved. Moreover, the one fully preserved Valentinian system that clearly proffers the model of deferred consolidation, the *Tripartite Tractate*, is somewhat problematic to use for this purpose. Consistent with its general habit of not attaching personal names to the agents in its mythological narrative, *Tri. Trac.* tells the story of the separation of the last aeon without naming either Sophia or Christos. Sophia is referred to simply as a certain "logos", and we are told that this logos suffered a "division" due to its inability to

---

[60] Cf. Thomassen, *Spiritual Seed*, 253–57. The name Christos for Sophia's son is not explicitly attested in the extant text of *Val. Exp.*

sustain the divine light.⁶¹ On the one hand, this logos reproduced itself as a unitary and perfect aeon, while on the other hand, its efforts to attain the Father himself gave rise to imitations, shadows and darkness. The perfect component of the logos hastened upwards and rejoined the Pleroma, whereas the defective part was left in the darkness below, afflicted by sickness and ignorance (77:11– 78:22). Although the names are left out, it is clear that *Tri. Trac.* is here alluding to the version of the Sophia myth which portrays her separation from the Pleroma as a split between Sophia and Christos. The "perfect part" "hastened upwards"⁶² and "abandoned"⁶³ the deficient logos in the same way that, according to the texts that present that version of the myth, Christos ascended to the Pleroma and abandoned his mother.⁶⁴ This particular motif of abandonment and ascent does not appear in the versions that describes the split as a duplication of Sophia herself.⁶⁵ It is specific to the Christos-Sophia variant of the myth.⁶⁶ The *Tripartite Tractate* assumes that variant, but rephrases it by resorting to a form of meta-language.

With due consideration for the imperfect nature of the evidence, I think it is a plausible conclusion that the Christos-Sophia version of the account of Sophia's separation from the Pleroma was typically associated with the model of deferred consolidation of the Pleroma both in the Gnostic and the Valentinian systems.

If we dare to ask the question of the chronological order of these versions, my working hypothesis would be that the version that associates Christos with the passion of Sophia is the older one, and that the "higher Christology" found in Irenaeus 1.29, the *Apocryphon of John*, and the major Valentinian systems preserved in the church fathers is the outcome of a later revision. I would further suggest that the motif of Christos' separation from Sophia, his abandon-

---

61 *Tri. Trac.* 77:18–21; we note here the same motif as with the First Woman in Irenaeus 1.30.1.
62 ⲁϥⲡⲱⲧ ⲁ₂ⲣⲏⲓ̈, 78:2; cf. 78:18–19, 23, 86:6, 8.
63 ⲁϥⲕⲱ, 78:4; ⲁϥⲕⲁⲁϥ, 78:18; cf. 80:24.
64 Iren. *Haer.* 1.11.1 ἀναδραμεῖν ... τὴν δὲ μητέρα ὑπολειφθεῖσαν; *Exc.* 23.2 καταλείψας ... εἰσελθών; 32.3 καταλείψας ... ἀνελθών; *Val. Exp.* 33:36–37 ⲛ̅ⲧⲁⲣⲉϥⲡⲱⲧ ⲁⲧⲡⲉ ⲁⲃⲁⲗ ⲛ̅ϩⲏⲧⲥ̅ ⲛ̅ϭ[ⲓ]ⲡⲉϥϣⲏⲣⲉ, cf. 33:22–23.
65 Cf. Iren. *Haer.* 1.2.4; [Hipp.] *Haer.* 6,31.4.
66 The motif reappears in Iren. *Haer.* 1.4.1 and [Hipp.] *Haer.* 6.31.7–8, where Christos, after having been produced by the Monogenes, takes pity on Achamoth/the lower Sophia, extends himself outside the Boundary, gives her (a first) formation, and then hastens back to the Pleroma. This episode clearly represents a secondary rewriting of the motif, made after the introduction of a different theory about the origin of Christos (Thomassen, "Relative Chronology," 21–23).

ment of her, and his ascent back into the Pleroma was modelled upon the historical event of the passion of Jesus, his separation from his body on the Cross, and his subsequent ascent. In other words, the story of Sophia's passion is an interpretation of the passion of Jesus. Finally, I would suggest that within the overarching context of a narrative of deferred consolidation, the passion of Jesus/Sophia is ultimately understood as an image of the infinite deity himself, whose act of self-manifestation, as he passes from boundlessness to determination, from unfathomability to knowability, from oneness to multiplicity, is perceived to belong in the category of suffering. The passion of Jesus, who embraced the multiplicity of the material world in order to teach humans about the true Father, represents a counterpart to this primordial act of compassionate divine manifestation.[67] In both cases, the state of divine suffering ends with a division and a detachment, through which the passion is eliminated. In the protological account, this takes place through the separation of Christos from Sophia; in the cosmic mission of Jesus, his passion comes to an end when his spirit is detached from his body on the Cross. For this reason, the Valentinians named the Boundary surrounding the Pleroma "the Cross": it represents the line of separation where the Saviour/Christos abandoned Sophia and her passion and returned to his place of origin.

This rather audacious interpretation of the passion story as a representation of the suffering the hidden deity himself inevitably submitted to once he decided to become known and to spread himself out into a Pleroma of multiple beings, belongs to the oldest stratum of Valentinian theology. It was subsequently modified by the constructors of the systems reported by the church fathers. I am now inclined to think that this interpretation did not originate with the early Valentinians, but was part of the legacy inherited from those "Gnostics" who Irenaeus claims were the "parents" of the Valentinians. The crucial piece of evidence for this hypothesis is the protology of the system in Irenaeus 1.30, in which the motif of the separation of Christos and Sophia is already attested. Alternatively, it may be argued that the system of 1.30 is itself influenced by

---

[67] The notion of divine passion is explicitly articulated in *Exc.* 29–31: the Father revealed himself to Silence out of compassion (συμπάθεια), which is a form of passion (πάθος). The whole Pleroma shared in the passion of Sophia; the descent of the Saviour into the world was a passion, and the aeons as well took part in this passion through the spiritual seed contained in the Saviour. These sections of *Exc.* clearly presuppose the model of deferred consolidation also found in the *Tripartite Tractate*. *Tri. Trac.* itself applies the concept of *sympatheia* to the Son, who manifests the Father by "extending himself" and "spreading out", language that evidently allude to the crucifixion (*Tri. Trac.* 65:4–23; cf. Thomassen and Painchaud, *Traité tripartite*, 305–7).

those early Valentinian theories. In my opinion, that possibility cannot be entirely eliminated at present. Nevertheless, a plausible scenario that emerges is that the Christos/Sophia passion motif as an element in the interpretation of the divine manifestation process is an archaic feature of Gnostic mythmaking that came to be revised at a later stage in the Barbelo Gnostic and Sethian tradition as well as in Valentinianism. In both these traditions, the motif was largely replaced, in parallel fashion, by a "higher" Christology that dissociated Christos from the passion of Sophia, and by the introduction of the model of pre-established consolidation. Perhaps the notion of a suffering deity who is restored to himself only at the end of world history and through the redemption of humans was too audacious to win general acceptance.

9 Conclusion

To conclude, the relationship claimed by Irenaeus between the "Gnostic sect" and the Valentinians has proved to be a fruitful point of departure for retracing historical coherence within a significant part of the field traditionally called "Gnosis". I think that Irenaeus was basically right: there *is* continuity between what he calls "the Gnostic sect" and the Valentinians, and I have here tried to reconstruct the main lines of that continuity. I have not gone into the many important ways in which the Valentinians changed the systems of their predecessors, for example by abandoning the figure of the evil world creator, the Protarchon, or Yaldabaoth, and replacing him with the much more benevolent Demiurge, and how they no longer chose to view the material world as a prison for the divine light, but rather as a place of growth for the spiritual seed. Describing those revisions, and attempting to account for the motives of the Valentinians in making them, would have to be the topic of another lecture.

At this point I should like, however, to comment on an age-old question that, to me at least, has appeared in a new light as a result of this investigation: the question of "the origins of Gnosticism". Granted that it is no longer fruitful to speak about "Gnosticism" in general terms, it should nonetheless be admissible to reflect on the sources of the specific ideas contained in Irenaeus 1.29 and 1.30 and further developed by the Valentinians. As noted above, the basic building blocks seem to derive from a peculiar exegesis of Genesis 1: the First Man, image of God, the Spirit, the Light. These terms were personified and combined in ways that one suspects were inspired by certain forms of contemporary Greek philosophy and allegorical Greek myth. Many scholars see this type of exegesis as having originated in a Jewish context, and maintain that the resulting myths were Christianised only at a later stage, once the Jews who invented them had come under the influence of Christianity.[68] As was pointed out above, however, the figure of Christos is an integral feature of these systems from the beginning. It cannot be regarded as a secondary addition to an already existing system. Thus, the assumption of other scholars that these myths arose within some form of Christianity is not to be discarded lightly.[69]

An objection that may be raised to this view is that it is difficult to see how this kind of thinking could have arisen out of the texts of the New Testament. Moreover, the figure of Christos, the anointed one, the Jewish Messiah, does not necessarily have to refer to Jesus of Nazareth. However, if I am right in seeing not only the figure of Christos himself, but also the story of his passion as a fundamental and primitive feature of the system, it becomes impossible not to assume that the myths presuppose the historical Jesus, whose suffering and death became the source of inspiration for a grandiose system of metaphysical speculation. If that system was constructed without any clear reference to the Christian ideas familiar to us from the New Testament, the explanation for that may very well be that those ideas had not yet acquired canonical status at the time when the system was originally conceived. Here, the observation made above, that early Gnostic texts typically took the form of treatises, takes on a particular significance: these treatises were written with no apparent concern, either in form or content, for the documents forming the later New Testament.

Whoever invented the original Gnostic system – and it is quite conceivable that it was the work of a specific individual unknown to us – was working simply from the fact of Jesus' passion, and on the assumption that the god Jesus called Father was a previously unknown deity far superior to the creator god of the Jewish scriptures. The gospels and the letters of Paul were not perceived as obligatory sources of reference – they were perhaps not even known to the writers of the first Gnostic treatises. With the Valentinians, that had changed; for them, authorisation derived from the texts of the gospels and Paul became important. Not so with their predecessors. In their case, we have to imagine a form of Christianity which is unlike any Christianity we know, and for which the name Christianity itself is an anachronism. The surviving testimonies of those

---

[68] Prominent scholars such as Birger Pearson, Kurt Rudolph, Hans-Martin Schenke and John D. Turner are among those have argued, in various ways, for this view. Instead of a full bibliography, I content myself with referring to the recent surveys by Lahe, *Gnosis und Judentum*, esp. 99–156; and Drecoll, "Martin Hengel"; Trompf, "Jewish Background."

[69] This position has been advocated in particular by Pétrement, *Le Dieu séparé*, and Logan, *Gnostic Truth* (cf. esp. 22, 30–32), though with arguments different from the ones offered here.

pre-Valentinian Gnostics give us a glimpse of the unknown territory of an early religion of the Christos, barely visible through the restricting lens of our preconceptions about what Christianity must look like.

Bibliography

Abbreviation

RD = Rousseau, Adelin, and Louis Doutreleau. *Irénée de Lyon: Contre les hérésies. Livre I/1–2* (SC 263, 264; Paris: Les Éditions du Cerf 1979); *Livre II/1–2* (SC 293, 294; Paris: Les Éditions du Cerf 1982); *Livre III/1–2* (SC 210, 211; Paris: Les Éditions du Cerf 1974); *Livre IV/1–2* (SC 100, 2 vols.; Paris: Les Éditions du Cerf 1965); *Livre V/1–2* (SC 152, 153; Paris: Les Éditions du Cerf 1969.

Literature

Bianchi, Ugo (ed.). *Le Origini dello gnosticismo: Colloquio di Messina 13-18 Aprile 1966*. SHR 12. Leiden: Brill 1970.
Brakke, David. *The Gnostics: Myth, Ritual, and Diversity in Early Christianity*. Cambridge, MA: Harvard University Press 2010.
Brox, Norbert. "Γνωστικοί als Häresiologischer Terminus." *ZNW* 57 (1966) 105–114.
Chiapparini, Giuliano. *Il divino senza veli. La dottrina delle 'Lettera valentiniana' di Epifanio, Panarion 31 5-6. Testo, traduzione e comment storico-religioso*. Studia patristica mediolanensia 29. Milan: Vita e pensiero 2015.
DeConick, April D. *The Gnostic New Age*. New York: Columbia University Press 2016.
Drecoll, Volker Henning. "Martin Hengel and the Origins of Gnosticism." In K. Corrigan and T. Rasimus (eds.), *Gnosticism, Platonism and the Late Ancient World: Essays in Honour of John D. Turner* (NHMS 82; Leiden/Boston 2013), 139–165.
Edwards, Mark. "Gnostics and Valentinians in the Church Fathers." *JTS* N.S. 40 (1989) 26–47. Repr. in M. Edwards, *Christians Gnostics and Philosophers in Late Antiquity* (Variorum Collected Studies Series; Farnham: Ashgate 2012), ch. IX.
Foerster, Werner. *Die Gnosis. 1: Die Zeugnisse der Kirchenväter*. 2nd ed. Zürich: Artemis & Winkler 1995.
Foerster, Werner. *Gnosis: A Selection of Gnostic Texts*. English translation edited by R. McL. Wilson. *I. Patristic Evidence*. Oxford: At the Clarendon Press 1972.
Halfwassen, Jens. *Auf den Spuren des Einen: Studien zur Metaphysik und ihrer Geschichte*. CM 14. Tübingen: Mohr Siebeck 2015.
Hanegraaff, Wouter J. (ed.). *Dictionary of Gnosis & Western Esotericism*. In collaboration with Antoine Faivre, Roeloef van den Broek, and Jean-Pierre Brach. Leiden/Boston: Brill 2006.
Harnack, Adolf. *Geschichte der altchristlichen Litteratur bis Eusebius. I: Die Überlieferung und der Bestand der altchristlichen Litteratur bis Eusebius*, bearb. unter Mitwirkung von Erwin Preuschen. 2 vols. Leipzig: Hinrichs 1893.
King, Karen L. *What is Gnosticism?* Cambridge, MA: Belknap Press of Harvard University Press 2003.
Krämer, Hans Joachim. *Der Ursprung der Geistmetaphysik: Untersuchungen zur Geschichte des Platonismus zwischen Platon und Plotin*. 2. Aufl. Amsterdam: B. R. Grüner 1967.
Lahe, Jaan. *Gnosis und Judentum: Alttestamentliche und jüdische Motive in der gnostischen Literatur und das Ursprungsproblem der Gnosis*. NHMS 75. Leiden/Boston: Brill 2012.

Layton, Bentley. "Prolegomena to the Study of Ancient Gnosticism." In L. Michael White and O. Larry Yarbrough (eds.), *The Social World of the First Christians: Essays in Honor of Wayne A. Meeks* (Minneapolis, MN: Fortress Press 1995), 334–350.

Layton, Bentley (ed.). *The Rediscovery of Gnosticism: Proceedings of the International Conference on Gnosticism at Yale New Haven*, Connecticut, March 28-31, 1978. Vol. 1: *The School of Valentinus*. Vol. 2: *Sethian Gnosticism*. SHR 41. Leiden: Brill 1980, 1981.

Logan, Alastair H.B. "The Development of Gnostic Theology with special reference to the Apocryphon of John, Irenaeus *adversus haereses* I 29 and 30, and related texts." PhD diss. University of St Andrews 1980.

Logan, Alastair H.B. *Gnostic Truth and Christian Heresy: A Study in the History of Gnosticism.* Edinburgh. T&T Clark 1996.

MacRae, George W. "The Jewish Background of the Gnostic Sophia Myth." *NovT* 12 (1970) 86–101. Repr. in id. *Studies in the New Testament and Gnosticism* (Good News Studies 26; Wilmington, DE: Michael Glazier Inc. 1987), 184–202.

Marjanen, Antti. "The *Apocryphon of John*, its Versions, and Irenaeus: What Have We Learned over 70 Years?" In E. Crégheur, L. Painchaud, T. Rasimus (eds.), *Nag Hammadi à 70 and. Qu'avons nous appris/Nag Hammadi at 70: What Have We Learned?* (BCNH.É 10; Peeters: Leuven 2019), 237–249.

Markschies, Christoph. *Valentinus Gnosticus? Untersuchungen zur valentinianischen Gnosis mit einem Kommentar zu den Fragmenten Valentins.* WUNT 65. Tübingen: Mohr Siebeck 1992.

Markschies, Christoph. "'Grande Notice': Einige einleitende Bemerkungen zur Überlieferung des sogenannten Systems der Schüler des Ptolemaeus Gnosticus." In C. Markschies and E. Thomassen (eds.), *Valentinianism: New Studies* (NHMS 96; Leiden/Boston: Brill 2019), 29–87.

McGuire, Anne Marie. "Valentinus and the 'Gnostike Hairesis': An Investigation of Valentinus' Position in the History of Gnosticism." Ph.D. Diss. Yale University 1983.

Painchaud, Louis. "The Literary Contacts Between the Writing Without Title *On the Origin of the World* (CG II,5 and XIII,2) and *Eugnostos the Blessed* (CG III,3 and V,1)." *JBL* 114 (1995) 81–101.

Pasquier, Anne. "Prouneikos. A Colorful Expression to Designate Wisdom in Gnostic Texts." In K. L. King (ed.), *Images of the Feminine in Gnosticism* (Studies in Antiquity & Christianity; Harrisburg, PA: Trinity Press International 2000), 47–66.

Pétrement, Simone. *Le Dieu séparé. Les origins du gnosticisme.* Paris, Les Éditions du Cerf 1984. Eng. tr. *A Separate God: The Christian Origins of Gnosticism.* Scranton, PA: HarperCollins 1990.

Quispel, Gilles. "Valentinian Gnosis and the Apocryphon of John." In Layton, *Rediscovery,* vol. 1, 118–132. Repr. in *Gnostica, Judaica, Catholica. Collected Essays of Gilles Quispel,* ed. J. van Oort (NHMS 55; Leiden: Brill 2008), 365–380.

Rasimus, Tuomas. *Paradise Reconsidered in Gnostic Mythmaking: Rethinking Sethianism in Light of the Ophite Evidence.* NHMS 68. Leiden/Boston: Brill 2009.

Schenke, Hans-Martin. *Der Same Seths: Hans-Martin Schenkes Kleine Schriften zu Gnosis, Koptologie und Neuem Testament.* Edited by G. S. Robinson, G. Schenke, and U.-K. Plisch. NHMS 78. Leiden: Brill 2012.

Schenke, Hans-Martin. "The Phenomenon and Significance of Gnostic Sethianism." In Layton, *Rediscovery,* vol. 2, 588–616. Repr. in Schenke, *Der Same Seths,* 501–528.

Schenke, Hans-Martin. "Nag Hammadi Studien I: Das literarische Problem des Apokryphon Johannis." *ZRGG* 14 (1962) 57–63. Repr. in Schenke, *Der Same Seths,* 33–39.

Schmid, Herbert. *Christen und Sethianer: Ein Beitrag zur Diskussion um den religionsgeschichtlichen und den kirschengeschichtlichen Begriff der Gnosis.* VCSup 143. Leiden/Boston: Brill 2018.

Schmid, Herbert. "Valentinianer und Gnostiker: Zu einer Bemerkung des Irenaeus von Lyon in *Adversus Haereses* 1.11.1." In C. Markschies and E. Thomassen (eds.), *Valentinianism: New Studies* (NHMS 96; Leiden/Boston: Brill 2019), 88–108.

Schmidt, Carl. "Irenäus und seine Quelle in *adv. haer.* I 29." In A. Harnack et al. (eds), *Philotesia. Paul Kleinert zum 70. Geburtstag dargebracht* (Berlin: Trowitzsch & Sohn 1907), 317–336.

Stead, G. C. "The Valentinian Myth of Sophia." *JTS,* N.S. 20 (1969) 75–104.

Thomassen, Einar. *The Spiritual Seed: The Church of the "Valentinians."* NHMS 60. Leiden: Brill 2006.

Thomassen, Einar. "The Melothesia of the Apocryphon of John and the Umm al-kitāb." In A. Van den Kerchove and L. G. Soares Santoprete (eds.), *Gnose et manichéisme: Entre les oasis d'Égypte et la Route de la Soie, Hommage à Jean-Daniel Dubois* (Bibliothèque de l'École des Hautes Études, Sciences Religieuses 176; Turnhout: Brepols 2017), 161–172.

Thomassen, Einar. "The Relative Chronology of the Valentinian Systems." In C. Markschies and E. Thomassen (eds.), *Valentinianism: New Studies* (NHMS 96; Leiden/Boston: Brill 2019), 17–28.

Trompf, Garry W., Gunner B. Mikkelsen, Jay Johnston (eds.), *The Gnostic World.* Routledge Worlds Series. Oxford: Routledge 2019.

Trompf, Garry W. "The Jewish Background of 'Gnosticism': A Guide for the Perplexed." In Trompf et al. *The Gnostic World,* 79–89.

Turner, John D. *Sethian Gnosticism and the Platonic Tradition.* BCNH.E 6. Québec: Les Presses de l'Université Laval/Louvain: Peeters 2001.

Van den Broek, Roelof. "Autogenes and Adamas." In id., *Studies in Gnosticism and Alexandrian Christianity* (NHMS 39; Brill: Leiden 1996), 56–66.

Waldstein, Michael, and Frederik Wisse. *The Apocryphon of John: Synopsis of Nag Hammadi Codices II,1; III,1; and IV,1 with BG 8502,2.* NHMS 33. Leiden: Brill 1995.

Williams, Michael A. Rethinking "Gnosticism": The Argument for Dismantling a Dubious Category. Princeton, NJ: Princeton University Press 1996.

www.ingramcontent.com/pod-product-compliance
Lightning Source LLC
Chambersburg PA
CBHW070310230426
43664CB00015B/2713